ATLANTA
ALIVE!

Ann Carroll Burgess

HUNTER

Hunter Publishing, Inc.
130 Campus Drive
Edison, NJ 08818-7816
☎ 732-225-1900 / 800-255-0343 / Fax 732-417-1744
Web site: www.hunterpublishing.com
E-mail: hunterp@bellsouth.net

IN CANADA
Ulysses Travel Publications
4176 Saint-Denis
Montreal, Québec H2W 2M5 Canada
☎ 514-843-9882, Ext. 2232 / Fax 514-843-9448

IN THE UK
Windsor Books International
The Boundary, Wheatley Road
Garsington, Oxford OX44 9EJ England
☎ 01865-361122 / Fax 01865-361133

ISBN 1-55650-911-1
© 2001 Hunter Publishing, Inc.

Maps by Lissa K. Dailey and Toni Carbone,
© 2001 Hunter Publishing, Inc.

4 3 2 1

About the Alive Guides

Reliable, detailed and personally researched by knowledgeable authors, the *Alive!* series was founded by Harriet and Arnold Greenberg.

This accomplished travel-writing team also operates a renowned bookstore, **The Complete Traveller**, at 199 Madison Avenue in New York City.

About the Author

Ann Carroll Burgess is a professional travel writer and broadcaster who has lived in Atlanta for nearly a decade. She currently hosts *Postcards*, a live call-in radio talk show that features interviews with travel-industry guests and reports on destinations.

Her work has appeared in magazines and newspapers in both Canada and the United States.

She also conducts seminars on travel writing and is a member of the Canadian Consulate's advisory board on tourism.

www.hunterpublishing.com

Hunter's full range of travel guides to all corners of the globe is featured on our exciting Web site. You'll find guidebooks to suit every type of traveler, no matter what their budget, lifestyle, or idea of fun. Full descriptions are given for each book, along with reviewers' comments and a cover image. Books may be purchased on-line using a credit card via our secure transaction system. All online orders receive 20% discount.

Alive! guides featured include: *Aruba, Bonaire & Curaçao*; *Antigua, Barbuda, St. Kitts & Nevis*; *Bermuda*; *Buenos Aires & The Best of Argentina*; *The Catskills*; *The Cayman Islands*; *Dallas & Fort Worth*; *Jamaica*; *Martinique, Guadeloupe, Dominica & St. Lucia*; *Miami & The Florida Keys*; *Nassau & The Best of The Bahamas*; *St. Martin & St. Barts*; and *Venezuela*.

Check out our *Adventure Guides*, a series aimed at the independent traveler who enjoys outdoor activities (rafting, hiking, biking, skiing, canoeing, etc.). All books in this signature series cover places to stay and eat, sightseeing, in-town attractions, transportation and more!

Hunter's *Romantic Weekends* series offers myriad things to do for couples of all ages and lifestyles. Quaint places to stay and restaurants where the ambiance will take your breath away are included, along with fun activities that you and your partner will remember forever.

To Barbara Rogers, who encouraged me
to do this project, and to Tom, who was
with me every step of the way.

Acknowledgments

This project would never have been achieved without the assistance of many knowledgeable associates and friends in the Atlanta community. I'd particularly like to thank Brandy Humphries of the Atlanta Convention & Visitors Bureau; Michael Brubaker of the Atlanta History Center; Frank Catroppa of the Martin Luther King Jr. National Park Historic Site; Kimberley Hartley of CNN; Megan Winokur of Zoo Atlanta; Linda Martin of the Atlanta Fulton Public Library; Tim Shannon of Pro-Active Public Relations; Kate Pilgrim; Sallie Cruise; and Pat Edwards.

We Love to Get Mail

This book has been carefully researched to bring you current, accurate information. But no place is unchanging. We welcome your comments for future editions. Please write us at: *Alive Guides*, c/o Hunter Publishing, 130 Campus Drive, Edison, NJ 08818, or e-mail your comments to hunterp@bellsouth.net. Due to the volume of mail we receive, we regret that we cannot personally reply to each letter or message, but your comments are greatly appreciated and will be read.

Contents

Sunup to Sundown

Maps

Introduction

Atlanta is not your usual run-of-the-mill tourist destination. There are no beaches on which to bask. No mountains on which to ski. No cobble-stoned quaintness or soaring gothic cathedrals.

What is Atlanta? It's a biplane ride for two over Stone Mountain at sunrise, cheering at a Braves game, cocktails at the Sun Dial more than 70 stories above Atlanta's skyline, Coca-Cola, CNN, Civil War encampments, ribs dripping with barbecue sauce, and much, much more.

Filled with a wealth of attractions and activities, metropolitan Atlanta offers something for almost every visitor. Some of Atlanta's well-known favor-ites include the Atlanta Cyclorama, CNN Studio Tours, Stone Mountain Park, the Martin Luther King, Jr. Historic District, Six Flags Over Georgia, and Zoo Atlanta.

For the culturally minded, metropolitan Atlanta museums highlight the arts, the Civil War, Atlanta and Georgia history, science and technology, and African-American history.

Visitors can study an impressionist painting or con-temporary sculpture at the High Museum of Art; enjoy the graceful Atlanta ballet, the oldest continu-ously operating ballet company in the nation; revel in a touring Broadway musical; or enjoy the Grammy award-winning Atlanta Symphony Orchestra.

For the more active tourist, activities include water and amusement parks, golfing, tennis, auto racing, train excursions and more. Sports fans can cheer on the Braves, the Falcons, the Hawks, or the Thrashers.

One glance at Atlanta's skyline and your visions of Scarlett and Tara will be "gone with the wind." But tucked in among the canyons created by the skyscrapers on Peachtree Street, you'll find the apartment home where Margaret Mitchell composed her blockbuster novel, within a brand new museum devoted to the film.

From its trend-setting restaurants and sky-scraping hotels to the ultra-modern sports facilities and oh-so-hip urban lofts, Atlanta symbolizes the "new South." A vibrant global player in industry, communications and the arts, the city never loses sight of its vivid, often turbulent history.

 # History

The legendary symbol of the phoenix of Egyptian mythology is an apt one for Atlanta; on more than one occasion, literally or figuratively, the city has risen from the ashes with renewed beauty and strength.

Early Settlers

The first known inhabitants of the area we call Georgia were prehistoric Indians referred to as **Mound Builders**. They were followed by the **Cherokee Indians**, who settled north and west of the Chattahoochee River, and the **Creek**, who populated the area to the south and east of the river.

The 1800s

European settlers, predominantly British, began arriving in the 18th century. The state was named in 1732 after Great Britain's King George II, and was the last of the original 13 colonies. During the war of 1812, the **British** built a small log fort at the junction of Peachtree Creek and the Chattahoochee River, on the site of an Indian village called "Standing Peachtree." From this site grew the city we call Atlanta.

Atlanta was a latecomer to the stage of history. Marietta, 20 miles to the North, was laid out in 1833; Decatur, to the east, got going in 1822. Savannah, Georgia's first city, was founded in 1733 and played an important part in the Revolutionary War.

It wasn't until 1837, when the Western & Atlantic Railroad selected the site to be the southern end of its tracks, that the city began taking on substantive shape. The town was called **Terminus** until 1843, when it was renamed **Marthasville**, after the daughter of Gov. Wilson Lumpkin. In 1847 it was christened **Atlanta**, supposedly a feminine form of "Atlantic," most likely created by an engineer with the Western & Atlantic.

★ **DID YOU KNOW?**

Before the city even had a name, it had a number, **Lot No. 77.** The Western & Atlantic Railroad considered this lot to be ideal for a depot and approached owner Samuel Mitchell to sell the property because of the state's need for it. In a show of generosity, Mitchell donated the lot to the state of Georgia.

Atlanta is the only major American city to have been destroyed by war.

By the time the Civil War began in 1861, Atlanta was a major railroad hub, manufacturing center and supply depot. In 1864, General William Sherman, during his infamous "March to the Sea," burned all of the railroad facilities, almost every business and more than two thirds of the city's homes, in an attempt to cripple transportation and supply lines.

Atlanta didn't lie in ruins for long. Within four years of Sherman's attack, the Georgia capital was moved from nearby Milledgeville, where it had been seated since 1804, to Atlanta, and the city launched its first campaign to attract new business. By 1877, telephone service was introduced into Atlanta, the *Atlanta Constitution* (still published daily) had been founded, Atlanta University had been chartered, and the Atlanta Chamber of Commerce organized.

Introduction

In 1895, this "brave and beautiful city," so called by newspaper editor Henry Grady, hosted the Cotton States and International Exposition in Piedmont Park, and showed 800,000 visitors that Atlanta was headed in new directions. One hundred and one years later, Atlanta would welcome the world to the 1996 Olympics.

The 1900s

By the end of the 1920s, Atlanta was ready to tackle new dimensions, and the first "Forward Atlanta" campaign brought more than 600 new businesses to the city. At the same time, visionary Atlanta Alderman (and later Mayor) William B. Hartsfield, worked vigorously to turn an unused racetrack into an airport. By 1929 the new airport was handling 16 passenger and mail flights a day. Today, Hartsfield Atlanta International Airport is among the busiest airports in the world.

In 1900, Atlanta University professor W.E.B. DuBois formed the NAACP.

By 1936, Margaret Mitchell had completed her book, and *Gone With The Wind* once again focused world attention on the city. The book won the Pulitzer

Prize in 1937, and in 1939 the movie had its world premiere in Atlanta.

In 1964, Martin Luther King, Jr. won the Nobel Peace Prize.

Following World War II, the city continued its economic surge and also became known as "the city too busy to hate." Atlanta and Georgia avoided much of the strife associated with the Civil Rights Movement, during the '50s and '60s, simply by taking the lead in securing minority rights. Native son **Dr. Martin Luther King, Jr.** is identified as the leader but many others played significant roles. Atlanta Mayor Ivan Allen, Jr. was the only Southern mayor to testify before Congress in support of the pending Civil Rights Bill. When Dr. King was assassinated in 1968, Mayor Allen pleaded for calm. The city met his request with peaceful, but anguished, mourning.

In 1965, the city of Atlanta built **Atlanta-Fulton County Stadium**, in spite of the fact that it hadn't signed a baseball team to play there. It wasn't long before the Braves moved from Milwaukee to the city. At the same time, the National Football league awarded the city the Falcons expansion team. Hank Aaron's historic home run number 715 occurred at the Atlanta-Fulton County Stadium in April of 1974.

★ DID YOU KNOW?

On September 18, 1990, thousands of Atlantans stayed away from work and school to listen to the International Olympic Committee make its announcement of the selection of the host city for the 1996 summer Olympics. Following the announcement by IOC Chairman Juan Antonio Samaranch that the games would go to "the city of Atlanta," approximately 50,000 people partied the day away at Underground Atlanta in celebration.

From July 20 through August 4, 1996, the eyes of the world were focused on Atlanta as the city welcomed the Centennial Olympic Games. The games served as a catalyst for even more economic resurgence by fueling more than $2 billion of construction and restoration projects.

If there is an Atlanta trademark, it is the constantly changing skyline. Atlanta's ability to grow and reinvent itself defines the city's personality – an assertive, dynamic metropolis that is marching boldly into the future.

The Olympic Legacy

The heart of downtown Atlanta today reflects the best of the city. From the glittering skyline to the 21-acre Centennial Park built for the 1996 Olympics, you'll discover a city on the edge of tomorrow. Little wonder that this is the home of CNN, Coca-Cola, Home Depot, Delta Air Lines, Georgia-Pacific, and UPS.

The Olympic flame that swept through Atlanta in the summer of 1996 continues to burn brightly. All of the painting, repairing and fixing up that Atlanta performed to smarten the city for Olympic visitors has carried well into the new millennium.

Even though the Olympics have come and gone, the building and improving continues. Centennial Park, with its undulating paths of commemorative bricks that encircle the shimmering Fountain of Rings, provides a foreground for Atlanta's dramatic skyline and a new public space for Sunday afternoons, Fourth of July celebrations, arts and crafts festivals and concerts.

★ DID YOU KNOW?

One of the many artscapes created during the Olympic renovation is John Wesley Dobbs Plaza, just east of the 1-75/I-85 overpass on Auburn Avenue. The plaza features a life mask of its namesake, J.W. Dobbs, grandfather of former mayor Maynard Jackson. Dobbs was largely responsible for the development of Auburn Avenue as Atlanta's "Black Wall Street."

The most striking new addition to downtown Atlanta is the Philips Arena, giving a much-needed new home to the Atlanta Hawks basketball team, and creating a nest for the new Atlanta Thrashers hockey franchise.

The nearby Georgia Dome, the domain of Olympic gymnastics and basketball, played host to Superbowl XXXIV in January of 2000, and is home to the Falcons, Atlanta's NFL entry.

Within view of these bright and shining additions to Atlanta are powerful monuments to Atlanta's history. The State Capitol, with its gleaming dome of Georgia gold, sits atop a hill that, in 1865, was occupied by General Sherman's troops. On Auburn Avenue, the Martin Luther King, Jr. Center for Non-Violent Social Change, near the assassinated civil rights leader's birthplace and the church where he preached, is a constant reminder of the ongoing quest for civil rights.

These juxtapositions of history and future are what help to define Atlanta's uniqueness. Underground Atlanta, with its hidden delights, marks the birthplace of the city; a few MARTA stops away, the Fox Theatre, an architectural riot of domes and minarets, reflects the excesses of the 1920s. Less than a mile north on Peachtree Street, the recently restored home of Margaret Mitchell is a diminutive museum of life in the 1930s sandwiched between business towers of the '90s. Continuing north on Peachtree Street, the High Museum of Art glistens with sleek white porcelain panels in the sun of a new millennium.

A little-known aspect of Atlanta is its growing international community. Along Buford Highway, a tapestry of Asian and Spanish-American cultures is evolving with amazing speed. Within a seven-mile span, visitors can rent Chinese videos, buy Vietnamese newspapers, shop in a Korean mall, and sample

Mexican or Costa Rican restaurants. Atlanta's official International Boulevard runs from Courtland Street to the World Congress Center. The "unofficial" international boulevard thrives between Lenox Road and the Gwinnett County line.

Atlanta's traditional roots and recent international arrivals have had a significant impact on the culinary aspects of the city. Southern hospitality has always evolved around good eating, and as the new millennium begins this doesn't appear to be in any danger of changing. New restaurants are being added to the city almost daily. From casual cafés to cutting edge eateries, this is a city that loves to eat.

For one brief shining Olympic summer, Atlanta was in the international spotlight. The show may be over, but the lights have not dimmed on this city of the future.

Atlantans Today

Scarlett doesn't live here anymore. This is a city composed of hardworking, generous, and globally aware citizens. Atlanta is Jimmy and Rosalynn Carter, Ted Turner and Jane Fonda. Atlanta is Matt Mosely, the fireman who rescued a worker from atop a crane caught in a roaring fire. Atlanta is baseball great Hank Aaron and photographer par excellence Harry Callahan.

Atlanta is Margaret Edson, the kindergarten teacher who won a Pulitzer prize for her first play, *Wit*, and went right back to teaching.

Scratch citizens of Atlanta and you'll find people who know how to triumph over adversity with imagination and ingenuity. Couple this with an unbridled sense of risk-taking and perseverance, and you have the recipe for a city that has sought and won the 1996 Olympics, NFL Superbowls, and Baseball's All Star Games. It's a city of ordinary folks whose determination and grit have turned them into extraordinary heroes.

Geography

Just Where is Atlanta?

Atlanta is located in the northern half of the state of Georgia, in an area known as the **Piedmont**. This is a region of undulating hills wedged between the rugged Appalachian Mountains and the flat coastal plain.

It was because of these geographic characteristics that Atlanta got its start as a transportation hub. The location was selected because it was the first place south of the mountains sufficiently flat to be viable as a connection point for railroads from the north, east, south and west. Remember, Atlanta's original name was Terminus.

The very same factors that made Atlanta such a desirable hub for railroads made it even more favorable for highways, airlines, and, eventually, the convention trade. Atlanta was, and is, a crossroads town.

Metropolitan Atlanta sprawls over an immense area encompassing 20 counties and approximately 100 cities and towns. More than three million people live and work in the area. Atlanta proper is a city of 136 square miles and 400,000 residents. Within the con-

Atlanta Area

1. Etowah Mounds State Historic Site
2. Kennesaw Mountain National Battlefield Park
3. Six Flags Over Georgia
4. Peachtree Creek Battle Site
5. Ezra Church Battle Site
6. Callaway Gardens
7. Jonesboro Battle Site

.... Central Atlanta Area

8. Chattahoochee Nature Center
9. Chattahoochee River Recreation Area
10. Emory University Area
11. Stone Mountain Park
12. Amicalola Falls State Park

✈ Hartsfield-Atlanta International Airport

fines of the Perimeter, a transportation band that encircles the city, you'll discover a diverse range of neighborhoods, each with its own personality.

Planning Your Trip

When To Visit

Spring and fall are the most pleasant times to visit Atlanta. In the spring, Atlanta is as pretty as any Southern belle could hope to be. The city blazes with blossoms of Bradford pear, white dogwood and pink azaleas. Fall is equally mild tempered and colorful, with maple, hickory and oak foliage adding a decorative touch until almost Christmas. Summer is hot, humid and languid. Air conditioning will save you from the heat, but be prepared for the city (with the exception of the traffic) to move at a leisurely pace.

During the second weekend of April, Atlanta has traditionally welcomed "Freaknik" (Black College Spring Break). The traffic jams can be phenomenal as the students "cruise" the city into the wee hours of the night.

Winters are generally mild but not completely snow free. The mere mention of a snowstorm is capable of bringing the city to a halt. If even a few flakes begin to fall, avoid the freeways. Atlanta drivers have no experience whatsoever with snow, and they turn the freeways into a bumper car ride.

Atlanta welcomes some of the largest trade shows and conventions in the world, and these take place throughout the year. If you are attempting to visit the city while any conventions are in progress, you can expect to find hotels rooms scarce and prices high.

ATLANTA WEATHER CONDITIONS				
Month	Temperature (Farenheit/Centigrade)		Precipitation (in inches)	
	High	Low	Rain	Snow
Jan.	52/11	32/0	4.24	1
Feb.	58/13	33/3	4.31	1
Mar.	66/16	45/5	5.84	T
Apr.	77/22	46/11	4.61	T
May	83/26	55/5	3.71	0
June	87/30	63/20	3.67	0
July	88/31	68/21	4.90	0
Aug.	88/31	67/21	3.54	0
Sept.	86/27	58/17	3.15	0
Oct.	78/23	46/11	2.50	0
Nov.	59/17	38/5	3.43	0
Dec.	58/12	35/1	4.24	T
T=Trace		Source: The Weather Channel		

What To Wear

If you are Atlanta-bound on business, be prepared to dress to the nines. This is a sophisticated city that wears a coat and tie even during the worst heat of the summer. For sightseeing, neat and casual is the order of the day. This is not a beach or resort destination; skimpy halter tops and barely-there shorts just won't do. Restaurants don't require a jacket and tie, except for the fanciest dining establishments.

Natural fibers such as cotton and linen are your best bets during the long, hot and humid summers. Try to avoid synthetic fibers, which do not breathe well in the heat. Because almost everything in Atlanta is air conditioned, you'll want to include a sweater or light jacket in your suitcase. As the winters can be very chilly and rainy, sometimes punctuated with snow flurries, it's wise to bring a raincoat with lining and an umbrella. Spring and fall are the most moderate of the seasons, but they can be unpredictable. Dressing in layers will be your best course of action.

Money Matters

If you are arriving from outside of the United States, try to obtain US currency prior to your arrival. Exchange bureaus are few and far between, even at airports. Outside of major cities you will find that they are almost nonexistent. It is best to avoid having to exchange money or travelers checks in foreign currency at all, because of steep transaction fees imposed by the banks. Almost all hotels, restaurants, auto rental companies, shops and attractions take major credit cards.

Cards commonly accepted in the United States include Visa, MasterCard (Eurocard in Europe, Access in Great Britain), American Express, Diners, and Discover. You must have a credit card in order to rent an automobile.

Telephone Connections

One of the side effects of Atlanta's burgeoning population is the demand for new area codes. Metro Atlanta now has three, and you must use an area code, but not the number 1, to dial within the city. You must do this even if you are calling within the same area code.

In general, but with a few exceptions, the area inside the I-285 perimeter highway, including Atlanta and Decatur, is assigned the **404** area code. A huge area outside I-285, stretching as far south as Newnan and as far north as Lake Lanier, uses the **770** area code. To add to the confusion, new telephone numbers in both areas are being assigned the **678** area code. It is possible for two numbers at the same address to have two different area codes.

⊚ TIP

Pay phones cost 35¢ and don't always give change, so you will need to have the correct amount if you want to avoid paying extra for the call.

Crime

Atlanta is a big city, complete with all of the urban problems of any large American city. The city has taken proactive steps to lessen these problems for the visitor by creating the downtown Ambassadors. This urban patrol group, initiated during the Olympics and affiliated with the police department, assists tourists with directions, and can even provide an escort to your hotel. The presence of this patrol has significantly reduced the number of crimes in the downtown area. The Ambassadors are readily recognized by their white pith helmets and teal green jackets emblazoned with a red and gold *A*; ☎ 404-215-9600.

Many areas in Atlanta change in the blink of an eye, or the walk of one block, from a relatively safe neighborhood to a danger zone. Take special care to keep your wits about you when venturing out on your own. If you are unsure of an area's personality, ask the hotel concierge for advice before roaming too far.

Holidays & Special Events

January

New Year's Eve Celebrations

New Year's is a huge event in Atlanta. Over 200,000 people generally gather at **Underground Atlanta** to mark the end of the old year and the beginning of the new with the dropping of the "Big Peach."

Other popular spots to celebrate the festivities include the **Sun Dial**, the rotating bar 70 stories above the city at the top of the Westin Peachtree Plaza Hotel, and the **Hyatt Regency Hotel**.

Families, and those interested in a nonalcoholic celebration, will enjoy First Night, which takes place in Midtown, along Peachtree Street between 14th Street and Pershing Point.

Be sure to book well in advance for New Year's Eve, as hotels fill up early.

> ⊚ **TIP**
>
> Upon arrival at your hotel be sure
> to ask the concierge for a copy of
> *Where Atlanta*, a monthly guide to
> what is happening in the city.

Atlanta Boat Show

The largest boat show between Miami and New
York, this event draws buyers for everything from
10-foot canoes to 85-foot yachts. Over 100,000 people attend, to see upwards of $10 million in boats.

Contact the organizers of the Great Southern Boat
Show at 1700 Geurgins Street, Norcross; ☎ 770-279-
0213.

King Week Celebrations

A week-long series of speeches, films, seminars and
music celebrating the birth of civil rights leader and
Nobel Prize recipient Dr. Martin Luther King, Jr.
begins with an interfaith service, and ends with a
parade down Auburn Avenue, with related events
throughout the city. The event usually begins on the
second weekend in January. For more information,
contact the **Martin Luther King, Jr. Center for
Nonviolent Social Change**, 449 Auburn Avenue NE, Atlanta, GA 30312; ☎ 404-526-8900,
www.thekingcenter.com.

February

Goodwill Book Sale

The largest used book sale in Atlanta begins the first
full week in February and lasts for over a week. Be

sure to arrive early on the first day for the best selection. Folks wait all year for this book sale, some even bringing their own shopping carts; ☎ 404-486-8499.

Southeastern Flower Show

Thousands of flowers in early bloom, lectures, demonstrations, gardens and landscaping are all part of this show. It's enough to make you want to play in the dirt again. The show is usually held around the last week of February at the Atlanta Expo Center, 3650 Jonesboro Road, SE (take Exit 55 off I-285). For information, call ☎ 404-888-5638; www.flower-show.org.

March

St. Patrick's Day Celebrations

The **Irish Hibernian Benevolent Society** of Atlanta has been sponsoring the downtown St. Patrick's Day parade for almost 120 years, making it the oldest continuing civic event in Atlanta. This is a down-home parade with an easygoing atmosphere. The **Buckhead Parade**, held on the Saturday closest to March 17th, is more of a hard-partying celebration, with the crowd retiring to the bars at its conclusion. ☎ 404-505-1208.

Atlanta Home Show

Anything that has to do with the good life at home in the south, you'll find here. The spring spring show is usually held in mid-March at the Georgia World Congress Center. ☎ 770-998-9800.

Civil War Relic Show

Visitors from the north might find that the perspective at this collectibles show is somewhat slanted to a Southern point of view. You'll find relics, weapons, books, clothing and other artifacts for sale. Atlanta State Farmers Market, Forest Park, ☎ 404-366-6910.

Spring Celebration at Callaway Gardens

Stay for the weekend! Callaway Gardens is a beautiful resort with facilities for golf, tennis, and fine dining.

If this isn't the top azalea show in the south, it certainly belongs in the top two. You can drive a six-mile trail of red, white, pink and purple blooms, "oohing and ahhing" at every turn. Callaway Gardens is located at Highway 27, Pine Mountain, GA, about 1½ hours south of Atlanta. ☎ 800-225-5292; www.callawaygardens.org. See page 231, for resort information.

April

Dogwood Festival

The dogwoods and azaleas bloom on a schedule all their own, which may or may not coincide with the festival schedules.

This is a week-long celebration that everyone hopes will coincide with the peak of dogwood season. The center of the celebration is Piedmont Park, which features outdoor music and an art festival. You'll even find dogs jumping for joy (and Frisbees) at this fest. Usually held the first week of April. Most events are free. ☎ 404-875-7275; www.dogwood.org.

Kennesaw/Big Shanty Festival

The festival features a re-enactment of the June, 1864 Battle of Kennesaw Mountain, which took place when Union General William T. Sherman marched from Chattanooga south to Atlanta. There are crafts, food and a downtown parade. The Kennesaw Civil War Museum is at 2829 Cherokee St. NW, Kennesaw; ☎ 770-427-2117. See page 83 for additional information.

May

Music Midtown

This outdoor music festival, usually held on the first weekend in May, has featured performers such as Santana, ZZ Top and the Steve Miller Band. Various locations around town; tickets are required. For information, call ☎ 404-872-1115, www.music-midtown.com.

Atlanta Jazz Festival

You might hear Wynton Marsalis, Ron Carter, or even Miles Davis perform at this festival, traditionally held over Memorial Day weekend at various locations throughout the city. Some events are free, others require an admission. On the days prior to the festival, some of the artists give free, brown-bag lunchtime concerts in Woodruff Park, at Marietta and Peachtree streets, Downtown. ☎ 404-817-6851; www.atlantafestivals.com.

For concerts in the park during the Atlanta Jazz Festival, be sure to bring a picnic and a blanket.

June

Georgia Shakespeare Festival

Held at the Miriam H. and John A. Conant Performing Arts Center on the grounds of Oglethorpe University, this event features three or four different Shakespearean plays, in both traditional and contemporary formats. During the festival, ticket holders are invited to picnic on the lawn around the

Conant Performing Arts Center starting about 90 minutes before each evening's performance. The festival runs through August; contact the center at 4484 Peachtree Road, ☎ 404-264-0020, www.ga-shakespeare.org.

July

July Fourth

Don't expect to find a discount rate on July Fourth for any hotel on Peachtree between Buckhead and Midtown; this is the route for the Peachtree 10K Race, and rooms are booked months in advance.

This all-day celebration begins in the early morning with the Peachtree Road Race. The 10K event is so popular that participants sign up several months in advance. It's fun just to watch 50,000 sweaty runners, packed shoulder-to-shoulder, jog down Peachtree Street. The best place to view the race is at "Heartbreak Hill," in front of Piedmont Hospital at Peachtree Street and Collier Road. For information call the Atlanta Track Club, ☎ 404-231-9600.

The day's festivities continue with a parade downtown, and conclude with fireworks held in various locations. Lenox Square hosts an outstanding fireworks display. Go early for the best seating. Another great location to view the fireworks display is Centennial Olympic Park. Or book a hotel room – the Marriott, Swissôtel and the Ritz all have rooms that provide a good view – but be sure to confirm that you will be able to see the fireworks from your assigned room!

National Black Arts Festival

A world-class event that draws participants from all over the United States and abroad. Concerts, plays, dance performances, book fairs and workshops are all a part of this event. At various locations throughout Atlanta; usually held the last week in July and first week in August. ☎ 404-730-7315.

Civil War Encampment

Over a hundred participants display and demonstrate Civil War weapons, tents, uniforms and camp life. It gets a little noisy with all that cannon firing. This event commemorates the Battle of Atlanta, fought in 1864. Stone Mountain Park, ☎ 770-498-5690, www.stonemountainpark.com. See *Sunup to Sundown*, page 71, for more information.

August

Georgia Mountain Crafts Fair

You might want to take a weekend and spend some time in the lovely town of Dahlonega (about 75 miles northeast of Atlanta on Highway 400/Route 19) to take in one of the state's largest mountain country fairs. This is a hybrid of both craft and country events with plenty of music, food, crafts and clogging. Dahlonega/Lumpkin County Chamber of Commerce, 13 S. Park Street, Dahlonega, 30533, ☎ 706-864-3711 or 800-231-5543; www.dahlonega.org.

September

Montreux Music Festival

Named for the Swiss city that began this tradition, the Montreux Music festival brings a week of jazz, soul, and folk music to Chastain and Piedmont Parks, beginning Labor Day weekend. Admission is free. ☎ 404-817-6815, www.atlantafestivals.com.

October

Scottish Festival & Highland Games

For current happenings in the city, check the listings in the free weekly newspaper Creative Loafing, *or the weekend leisure guide of* The Atlanta Journal-Constitution.

The Atlanta Scottish clans and associated Gaelic groups congregate at Stone Mountain to pipe and drum, show off their kilts, folk dance and throw hammers and logs. The three-day event is usually held the third weekend in October. Admission fee to the park is all that is required. ☎ 770-521-0228.

Halloween

Atlanta loves to party, whether it's New Year's Eve, St. Patrick's Day or the Fourth of July. Halloween is just one more reason to celebrate. Buckhead and Little Five Points thrive with activity.

> ⊚ **TIP**
>
> Parking can be a nightmare at many of the festivals and events; whenever possible, take MARTA to your destination.

November

The Lighting of the Great Tree

A long-standing tradition in the city, this event is held Thanksgiving evening at Underground Atlanta. Brass bands and colorfully gowned choirs herald the opening of the Christmas season in Atlanta. ☎ 770-913-5551.

December

Callaway Gardens Fantasy In Lights

Visitors ride through six miles of Christmas lights arranged in themed sections. You must book tickets in advance for this popular attraction, which includes a Christmas village, crafts, nightly dinners at the Fantasy Café, a New Year's Eve dinner dance, and the Fantasy in Lights Bed & Breakfast. ☎ 800-(225-5292), www.callawaygardens.org.

Festival of Trees

This popular event at the Georgia World Congress Center has spawned similar festivals in other part of the country. Designers, school groups, garden clubs and other sponsors trim over 200 trees with imaginative decorations. Proceeds from the ticket sales go to the Eggleston Children's Hospital in Druid Hills. ☎ 404-325-NOEL.

Plan to spend at least two hours at the Festival of Trees to give the kids a chance to ride on the "pink pig," a rite of Christmas in the city.

Christmas at Callanwolde

The former home of Charles Howard Candler, son of Coca-Cola founder Asa Candler, is decorated by designers to celebrate the season. A lovely way to get into the spirit of Christmas past as you walk from one room to another within this attractive period home. This is a 24-year tradition that involves three million lights, holiday shops, a café, a breakfast with Santa, and an opening night Black Tie Premiere to kick off the seasonal event. Tickets are required; ☎ 404-872-5338, www.callanwolde.org (see *Sunup to Sundown*, page 81, for additional information about the Callanwolde Fine Arts Center).

A special feature of Christmas at Callanwolde is the music played on the home's massive 3,752-pipe, 20,000-pound Aeolian organ, the largest of its kind still in playable condition.

The Peach Bowl

This major football event in the city draws people not only for the game, usually played around December 29th, but for the New Year's celebrations. ☎ 404-586-8500.

Where To Stay

Atlanta is blessed with an extensive array of options from which to select. Your choice of hotel or bed-and-breakfast should be based on what you have planned for your stay. If you are convention-bound at a location downtown or at the Georgia World Congress Center (GWCC), you will save tremendous amounts of time by staying near the venue to avoid traveling during peak rush hours.

Have you come to shop? A hotel in Buckhead or a suburban location will place you at the epicenter of fashion and nightlife.

If you have come to visit as a tourist and expect to be driving to locations outside the downtown or perimeter area, then a suburban location, with its reduced prices, is a good choice.

Alive Price Scale

Prices are always subject to change. For a major North American city, you will find Atlanta prices to be quite reasonable. Rather than specific prices, the *Alive Guide* uses price levels to provide you with guidelines. For the attractions, we've indicated which ones charge admission and those that are free.

Hotel rates are difficult to quote because of the variance in accommodations; the prices for standard, deluxe, garden view, etc., all factor into what a hotel will charge for any particular room on any particular night. The pricing scale for hotels is based on the rate for a double room.

ACCOMMODATIONS PRICE SCALE
Inexpensive . . . . $50-$100
Moderate . . . . $100-$150
Expensive. . . . . $150-$200
Deluxe . . . . .More than $200

For dining, the scale is based on the cost of an average entrée. Cocktails and wine are additional. Price estimates are per person.

DINING PRICE SCALE
Price scale reflects the cost of an average entrée.
Inexpensive . . . . $5-$10
Moderate . . . . $10-$25
Expensive. . . . . $25-$50
Deluxe . . . . .more than $50

Getting Here

Atlanta is the transportation hub of the South. You have probably been to Atlanta, if only en route to somewhere else, if you were flying to destinations in the Southeast.

By Air

If you fly, you will find that **Hartsfield Atlanta International Airport** is one of the easiest-to-use airports in the world. Taxis, rental car companies, and Atlanta's rapid rail system, MARTA, connect the airport with Downtown. Hartsfield Atlanta is about 10 miles south of Downtown, from either I-75, I-85, or I-285.

Hartsfield Atlanta International airport is one of the largest anywhere. To travel between concourses and the main terminal and baggage claim area, you can use either the airport rail or the moving sidewalks. For airport information, call ☎ 404-530-6830.

Be sure to allow at least 30 minutes of travel time between the airport and Downtown. You will find all of the ground transportation, including shuttle buses, rental car companies, taxis and limos operating from the west exit, just a few steps from the north terminal baggage claim area. The MARTA station is also located in this area.

Airport Transportation

The easiest and fastest way to travel between the airport and Downtown or Buckhead, is via **MARTA**, the rapid rail system. The fare is $1.50 one way; it takes approximately 20 minutes to reach Downtown and 30 minutes to arrive in Buckhead. Service operates from 5 am to 1 am, and it is a clean and safe service. ☎ 404-848-5389.

MARTA is handicapped-accessible. Lift vans are available for passengers with disabilities, and door-to-door service is offered between destinations and rapid rail stations. For handicapped services, call ☎ 404-848-5389.

Atlanta Airport Shuttle vans and buses operate from the airport at regular intervals between 7 am and 11 pm. The fare to Downtown is $10 one way, or $17 round trip, and takes about 20 minutes, with stops at the major hotels. To Buckhead, the fare is $15 one way, $24 round trip. Service is also available to Emory University and Lenox Square Mall.

Best bet transfer from the airport to Downtown, Midtown or Buckhead is MARTA.

Many hotels close to the airport operate their own van service, so be sure to check with your hotel.

Taxi fare between the airport and Downtown is fixed at $18 for one person, $20 for two people, and $24 for three to five persons. The fare to hotels in Buckhead and the Lenox Square area is $28 for one person, $30 for two or more persons. The trip takes about 30 minutes, depending upon traffic.

If you plan to stay within the city and do not want to rent a car, you will find that many of the city's hotels are within walking distance of a MARTA station.

By Car

If you drive, you will most likely enter Atlanta on one of three interstate highways that converge in the city, **I-75**, **I-85**, or **I-20**. These roads are all linked by a 63-mile perimeter road, **I-285**, that encircles the city. Unless absolutely necessary, avoid arriving during rush hours. Traffic clogs all of the freeways both morning and evening, and you cannot escape it.

"Spaghetti Junction" is the tangle of concrete at the northeast intersection of I-85 and I-285.

Parking in Atlanta is generous and relatively easy to find. Most hotels outside of the Perimeter have free parking for guests though you may have to pay a parking fee at hotels inside the Perimeter.

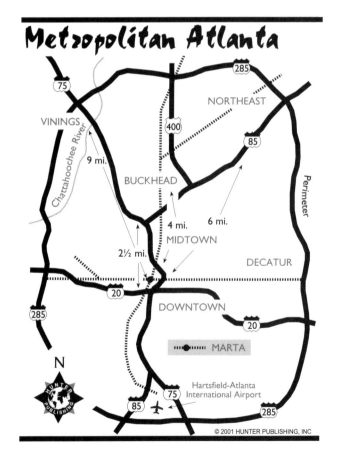

Metropolitan Atlanta

Regardless of how you choose to arrive in Atlanta, you may find it more convenient to have a car if you wish to travel outside the city. Attractions such as Stone Mountain and Six Flags Over Georgia are some distance from the city, and not conveniently reached by public transportation. For car rental information, see page 239.

Introduction

DRIVING TIPS & REGULATIONS

◎ The driver and all front-seat passengers of every car must wear a seat belt. Children aged four-18 must wear a seat belt, and those younger than four must ride in an approved safety seat.

You must be 21 or over to rent a car.

◎ You may make a right turn on a red light after a full stop, traffic permitting.

◎ Your headlights must be on (day or night) when you are driving through rain, fog, snow or smoke.

◎ If you can steer it, clear it. If you are involved in a minor accident, Georgia law requires that the vehicles be removed from the roadway immediately.

◎ Atlanta drives quickly; be prepared to blend with the traffic as you enter the freeway.

◎ Keep a sharp lookout for pedestrians, particularly in the Downtown and Buckhead areas; jaywalking is rampant.

◎ Inclement weather, either summer thunderstorms or icy winter conditions, can double any driving time. A good rule of thumb is three to four minutes to travel one mile.

By Bus

If you are arriving by bus, the **Greyhound** terminal is located on 232 Forsyth Street; ☎ 404-584-1731. From there, the nearest MARTA is the Gwinnett station.

By Rail

If you are arriving via rail, MARTA bus #23 stops just outside the **Amtrak** Brookwood Station at 1688 Peachtree Street NW. The #23 bus will take you either north to the Lenox MARTA station or south to the Arts Center station. For additional Amtrak information, call ☎ 404-881-3062, or 800-872-1477.

 # Getting Around

Orientation

An eagle eye (or satellite) view of Atlanta would reveal a city encircled by a highway, and divided by interstate roads into pie-shaped pieces. The encircling road is known as "the Perimeter." In Atlanta you either live inside or outside of the Perimeter. Outside is best defined as suburbia. Inside is hip, trendy and surprisingly filled with aging baby boomers who are abandoning suburbia and its lawn-mowing weekends for maintenance-free condos and lofts.

> ### ★ DID YOU KNOW?
>
> Visitors to Atlanta like to joke that every other street is called **Peachtree**. Believe it or not, there was once a brief campaign to erase the name entirely.

Peachtree is the street where Coca-Cola first fizzed and Atlanta's first Black millionaire set up shop. This is where Henry Grady and Margaret Mitchell lived and wrote and died. Where generations have listened to the Atlanta Symphony, admired paintings at the High, and watched movies at the Fox. This is where multitudes turned out to cheer Jefferson Davis and Franklin D. Roosevelt, Bobby Jones and the Braves, the peg-legged veterans of the battle of Peachtree Creek and the marathon runners of the Centennial Olympic Games. Almost 100 streets in Atlanta now contain the word "Peachtree" in their names. They appear in more than 15 counties. There are so many Peachtrees, in fact, that some local governments discourage creating new ones. Yet, "Peachtree" happens. And why not?

Peachtree is more than just the name of Atlanta's main street. Peachtree is a microcosm of the city's present and an archive of its past. Peachtree is the heart of Atlanta.

Today's Peachtree begins in the southern end of Downtown and rides a ridge north before turning east and bursting into a confusion of peachtree-something roads near the Perimeter.

Should you step off Peachtree you will find distinctive neighborhoods nestling among the trees only yards from this major thoroughfare.

Public Transportation

MARTA (Metropolitan Atlanta Rapid Transit Authority) is Atlanta's mass transit system that includes both light rail and bus services. The light-rail component of the system operates 240 electric rail cars on 46 miles of track, with 36 stations spread along its two lines. Although MARTA rail service is limited to east-west and north-south routes, you will find excellent bus connections at the stations. The bus service and routes are quite comprehensive and

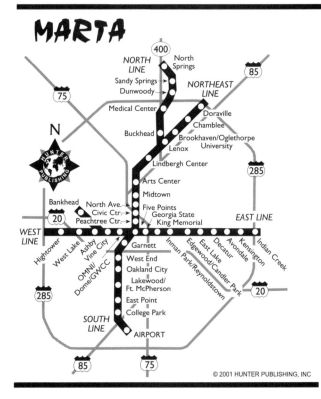

© 2001 HUNTER PUBLISHING, INC

there are very few locations in Atlanta which cannot be reached by MARTA.

Weekdays, trains operate every four to eight minutes between 5 am and 7 pm, and every 10 minutes from 7 pm until 1 am. On Saturdays, the trains operate every 10 minutes until 7 pm, and every 15 minutes from 7 pm until 1 am. Sundays and holidays, trains run every 15 minutes from 5 am to 12:30 am.

Bus schedules vary, but you can obtain a printed timetable for each and every route at the Five Points or Lindbergh Stations. Drivers usually have a supply of schedules for their individual routes.

> ## ⊚ TIP
>
> MARTA rail and bus schedule information is available by phone from 6 am-10 pm, Mondays to Fridays, and from 8 am-4 pm on Saturdays, Sundays and holidays; ☎ 404-848-4711. Just tell the operator your location and destination, and they will tell you which bus to take, where to catch it and if you need to transfer.

A single fare is currently $1.50 for each passenger older than three years of age. This fare includes two transfers. For example, you can ride MARTA from the airport to the Five Points Station, change to the other line, ride to another station and then get on a bus, all for a single fare. However, you cannot use a transfer as your return fare in a round-trip.

MARTA turnstiles accept tokens and transit cards. If you have neither, there are machines that accept paper currency and provide tokens and change. Be sure to have small bills if you don't need a lot of tokens or a massive amount of quarters in change.

MARTA's 20-pack of tokens for $25 is a good deal. You will save 25¢ on each fare, which is normally $1.50 per ride, including two transfers.

MARTA offers two kinds of transportation passes, other than tokens. The first is a monthly pass at $45 that provides unlimited rides. The second is the Transcard, at $12, for unlimited transportation Monday through Sunday. The weekly Transcard is good for a calendar week only. If you purchase it on a Wednesday you will only have five days to travel. The monthly card is issued for a calendar month.

Each of the MARTA stations has its own individual personality, style and architecture. The most intriguing is the Peachtree Center station, which was blasted out of the solid granite ridge under Peachtree Street. To get to the train platform at this station you will ride down one of the longest escalators in the southeast (don't worry, there is an elevator available!). The exposed surface of the granite creates a cave-like effect, enhanced by the knowledge that you are 12 stories below street level.

When the airport MARTA station opened in 1988, Atlanta became one of the few cities in the United States to offer direct rail service from the airport to Downtown. The fastest way to and from the airport is MARTA. In late 1999 Delta Air Lines opened a check-in facility in the MARTA station, making it even easier to use the rail system to the airport.

All MARTA trains and buses have "reserved" seats for the elderly and the handicapped. Almost all of MARTA's buses are handicapped-accessible and have wheelchair lifts. MARTA also operates L-Vans, which provide door-to-door service for the elderly or handicapped. A single fare for these buses is $3. For more information on this service, call ☎ 404-848-5389.

Sightseeing Tours

One of the best ways to maximize your time in Atlanta is to avail yourself of one of the many tours that combine historical and modern Atlanta. Check with the following tour operators for schedules and rates.

Taxis

To hail a cab in Atlanta, it's easiest to telephone or walk to a major hotel, where taxis congregate. Fares start at $1.50 for the first 1/7 mile, plus 20¢ for each additional 1/7 mile. Within the Downtown Convention Center zone, a flat rate of $5 for one or two persons is charged for any destination. Taxi companies are listed on page 240.

A large percentage of Atlanta's cabbies are from outside the country and many have difficulty with English and the geography of the city. Be prepared with good directions.

Walking Tours

ATLANTA PRESERVATION CENTER
156 Seventh Street NE, Suite 3
☎ 404-876-2040

The Center offers walking tours of many of Atlanta's neighborhoods. A tour with a guide is the best way to view many of the areas of Atlanta, as it is easy to wander into a less than desirable neighborhood. Some tours that you might consider are **Sweet Auburn**, the neighborhood associated with Martin Luther King, Jr.; **Inman Park**, the city's Victorian sweetheart; **Druid Hills**, of *Driving Miss Daisy* fame; and the **Fox Theatre**, the elaborate theater palace in Midtown.

PIEDMONT PARK CONSERVANCY
☎ 404-875-7275

The Conservancy offers a tour of historic Piedmont park on Saturdays, April through October.

Bus Tours

AMERICAN COACH/GRAY LINE OF ATLANTA
Tour Office: Underground Atlanta
65 Upper Alabama Street
Atlanta, GA 30303
☎ 404-767-0594

This is the largest charter carrier in Atlanta, featuring video-equipped coaches seating 45 to 55, minibuses, and two-door transit buses with or without wheelchair lifts. Radio-dispatched, specializing in shuttles, transfers, day-trips and extended tours.

AMERICAN SIGHTSEEING ATLANTA
550 Pharr Road, Suite 305
Atlanta, GA 30305
☎ 404-233-9140 or 800-572-3050

Daily sightseeing tours in a comfortable mini bus with a professional guide. No driver-guides. Bilingual interpreters are available for an additional fee.

CLASSIC TOURS AND DESTINATIONS

250 Auburn Avenue, Suite 305
Atlanta, GA 30303
☎ 404-589-1002 or 888-767-TOUR

Daily heritage sightseeing tours with hotel pickup. Customized city tours, educational tours, and step-on guides.

CIVIL WAR TOURS, INC.

2684 Canna Ridge Circle, NE
Atlanta, GA 30345
☎ 770-908-8410 or 888-678-8942

This company provides the only guided Civil War battlefield tours in the Atlanta area. These tours have been designed with the Civil War enthusiast in mind. Experience the life of a common soldier through the "Soldier Life" demonstration.

Neighborhoods & Communities

Inside the Perimeter

Downtown

For years, Downtown was the place to work, not live. The 1996 summer Olympics changed all that. New sculptures, attractive street lights, and landscaping have encouraged Downtown migration. The downtown Ambassadors (see page 16) patrol the streets offering security and assistance. Affiliated with the police, they keep the area rid of potential horrors. Old abandoned buildings, and former downtown businesses like the William Oliver building and the King Plow Arts Center (a renovated factory) have been converted into spacious loft apartments and

Downtown Atlanta

1. SciTrek
2. Civic Center
3. Centennial Olympic Park
4. GWCC
5. Georgia Dome
6. Chamber of Commerce
7. Philips Arena
8. CNN Center
9. Underground Atlanta
10. World of Coca Cola
11. Turner Field & Braves Stadium
12. State Capitol & Museum
13. Georgia State University
14. MLK, Jr. Historic District
15. Cyclorama
16. Zoo Atlanta
Ⓟ Parking
······■···· MARTA
☐ Five Points Station
NI Peachtree Center Station
N2 Civic Center Station
SI Garnett Station
WI OMNI/Dome/GWCC
EI Georgia State Station
E2 King Memorial Station

businesses. This new breed of housing has encouraged the young, artistic crowd to flock to the downtown area. The proximity to the Atlanta Convention Center, CNN, Georgia Dome, Philips Arena, restaurants, nightlife, art and cultural events creates a thriving, lively neighborhood.

Midtown

Just north of Downtown is the city's cultural center and enclave for singles, young professionals and the alternative lifestyle crowd. Midtown is aptly named for its location, being the midpoint between Downtown and Buckhead.

Midtown's special appeal is that it is the very heart of art and culture in Atlanta. The Woodruff Arts Center, housing the Atlanta Symphony and Alliance Theatre is adjacent to the High Museum of Art, at Peachtree and 15th Streets. Merely two blocks distant you'll find the 14th Street Playhouse, housing several independent theater companies.

The highlight of Atlanta's literary and cultural history is the recently restored Margaret Mitchell House, home of Atlanta's famous author at Peachtree and 10th Street.

Midtown also is home to Piedmont Park, Atlanta's weekend gathering place, where in good weather you will find walkers, bicyclists, and rollerbladers filling the park. Many of Atlanta's most important festivals and concerts are held here.

Buckhead

Buckhead is one of Atlanta's most prestigious neighborhoods, located north of Midtown. There are two faces to Buckhead; one is the residential aspect that has more than 100 private homes valued at over a

Midtown Atlanta

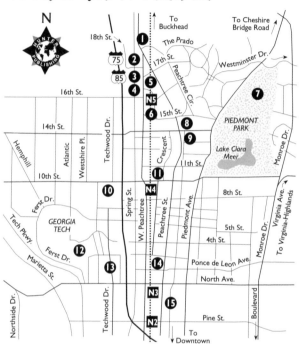

1. Rhodes Hall
2. William Breman Jewish Heritage Museum
3. Center for Puppetry Arts
4. Atlanta Ballet
5. High Museum of Art
6. Woodruff Memorial Arts Center
7. Atlanta Botanical Garden
8. Goethe Institute
9. 14th Street Playhouse
10. Alexander Memorial Coliseum
11. Margaret Mitchell House
12. Robert Ferst Center for Performing Arts
13. Bobby Dodd Stadium/Grant Field
14. Fox Theatre
15. Atlanta Preservation Center

···**N**··· MARTA Line and Stations

N2 Civic Center Station

N3 North Avenue Station

N4 Midtown Station

N5 Arts Center Station

Buckhead

██▓ MARTA

NE6 Lindbergh Center Station
NE7 Lenox Station
N7 Buckhead Station

1. Governor's Mansion
2. Atlanta History Center
3. Swan House
4. Peachtree Battle Park
5. Phipps Plaza
6. Lenox Square

© 2001 HUNTER PUBLISHING, INC

Introduction

million dollars each, sequestered in rolling dogwood and magnolia-covered hills; the other is its very public nightlife profile. This is where Atlanta goes to play at night. The bars are open into the wee hours, the restaurants are plentiful, and the shopping will do severe damage to your credit cards.

Buckhead is also home to the Governor's Mansion, the Atlanta Historical Society, the Historic Swan House and the Atlanta History Center.

Druid Hills

Druid Hills is one of the most successful and affluent residential communities in Atlanta, and is listed on the National Register of Historic Places. You'll find it curiously familiar if you have seen the film *Driving Miss Daisy*. Curving, winding roads circle around the Tudor, Georgian and traditional style two-story homes. Many of these elegant mansions are situated on large manicured slopes, surrounded by magnolias and dogwoods. Druid Hills is located close to Emory University and downtown Atlanta. This is where you'll find the Fernbank Museum and IMAX Theater, and Emory Village.

Little Five Points

Named after the Five Points intersection between Moreland, Euclid and McLendon avenues, Little Five Points is Atlanta's area of eclectic dining, shopping and artistic creativity, reminiscent of New York's Greenwich Village or Melrose Avenue in Los Angeles. This is the place to go if you can't leave town without a tattoo, body piercing or an evening in an alternative atmosphere.

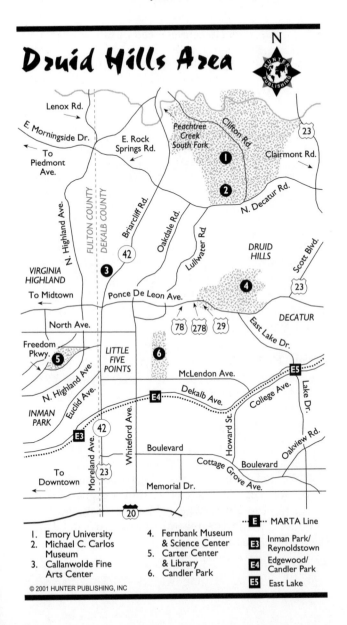

Druid Hills Area

N

1. Emory University
2. Michael C. Carlos Museum
3. Callanwolde Fine Arts Center
4. Fernbank Museum & Science Center
5. Carter Center & Library
6. Candler Park

E ··· MARTA Line

E3 Inman Park/ Reynoldstown

E4 Edgewood/ Candler Park

E5 East Lake

© 2001 HUNTER PUBLISHING, INC

Inman Park

Just west of Little Five Points is Atlanta's quintessential example of restoration. Inman Park, Atlanta's first planned suburb, was built in the early 1900s and originally was connected to the downtown area by trolley cars. The neighborhood was named for Edward H. Inman, original owner of the Swan House, located at the Atlanta History Center.

Unfortunately, during the mid-1900s the area became depressed and was virtually abandoned. Many of the once-beautiful homes fell into the hands of derelicts and transients.

In the early 1970s Inman Park became a center of urban gentrification and has been restored as one of Atlanta's premier residential areas. The streets, lined with shady willow trees, provide an almost pastoral background to the Victorian-style homes, many with gazebos and scalloped awnings.

Grant Park

To the east of I-75/I-85, in the neighborhood of Zoo Atlanta, is Grant Park, one of Atlanta's oldest neighborhoods, built between 1895 and 1915. Like Inman Park, Grant Park became a center of restoration during the 1970s.

Sweet Auburn

To the west of Inman Park is Atlanta's most racially integrated neighborhood, centered around Auburn Avenue. Called the Sweet Auburn district, this area is a popular residential area for African-Americans.

The area is noted for having been the center of black nightlife during a time when African-Americans

Introduction

Martin Luther King, Jr. Historic District

N

1. Visitors Center
2. Ebenezer Baptist Church
3. MLK, Jr. Gravesite
4. MLK, Jr. National Historic Site
5. MLK, Jr. Birth Home
6. APEX Museum
7. Auburn Avenue Research Center
8. Georgia State University
9. State Capitol

E1 GA State Station

E2 King Memorial Station

□ Five Points Station

P Parking

····■···· MARTA

© 2001 HUNTER PUBLISHING, INC

were restricted from frequenting white-owned businesses.

Today, Auburn Avenue is the center of Atlanta's African-American history, and features the Martin Luther King, Jr. Center for Nonviolent Social Change, the Martin Luther King National Park Service Visitors Center, King's birth home and Ebenezer Baptist Church, where King and his father preached.

This area underwent extensive renovations just prior to the 1996 Olympic Games.

Ansley Park

One of Atlanta's most popular neighborhoods, located just north of Midtown, is Ansley Park. The neighborhood began construction in 1905 as Atlanta's first automobile-oriented community and became one of Atlanta's premier residential areas. At one time the governor's residence was at 205 The Prado.

Wedged between two of Atlanta's busiest streets, Peachtree and Piedmont, the Ansley Park area is an oasis of almost pastoral beauty within the confines of the city. The entire neighborhood is listed in National Historic District Register.

The Ansley Park area is probably one of the most convoluted neighborhoods in Atlanta, and only the brave should venture out without a map and compass, or a long-time resident as guide.

Virginia-Highland

Virginia-Highland takes its name for the intersection of Virginia and North Highland avenues, to the east of Piedmont Park. This district is a popular spot for Atlanta's young professionals. At one time this prime area was in danger of becoming part of a planned highway system, but the efforts of community leaders and activists prevented that.

The neighborhood is an eclectic mix of older homes, smaller bungalows, and homes divided for apartment living. Noted for its renovations of older homes, shopping district, and one-of-a-kind eateries, this area has great charm and drawing power.

Virginia-Highland is the perfect place to go for a day's shopping or a leisurely stroll. It's even better at night, becoming the second most popular nightlife destination in Atlanta. Parking is scarce, especially at night, but you'll find the area accessible to most major expressways.

Decatur

Situated just six miles east of Atlanta, Decatur gives the appearance of being an Atlanta suburb, but in fact it is a separate town that predates Atlanta by 13 years. Decatur is known for its historic town square and stately homes. It is also the home of the Centers for Disease Control (CDC), Emory University, and the Carter Presidential Center.

Outside the Perimeter

Alpharetta

A particularly pretty bedroom community, located approximately 25 miles north of Atlanta on GA 400/Highway 19, Alpharetta has managed to preserve some of its historic main street. Here you can find antique shops, art galleries and coffee shops.

Marietta

A large community, northwest of Atlanta, which still has the flavor of a small Southern town, despite the bustling economic growth. The town was occupied by Union troops during the Civil War, and was spared the destructive forces of Sherman's troops in their march to the sea.

You'll discover neighborhoods of 19th-century Victorian homes, antebellum mansions, and modest bungalows. Marietta is also home to "The Big Chicken," a well-known landmark. Don't be surprised to be given directions that include "go past The Big Chicken."

The Square is the epicenter of Marietta's historic and cultural life, complete with shops, buildings of yesteryear, the Marietta/Cobb Museum of Art and the Theatre In The Square, .

Roswell

Settled at about the same time as Buckhead in the late 1830s, and located about 20 minutes north of downtown Atlanta, Roswell's historic area is well known for its antebellum homes. Named for Roswell King, a well-to-do planter, the town began its life as a cotton mill on the banks of the Chattahoochee River. The community eventually developed around the mill, and it wasn't long before large Tudor, Georgian and Colonial mansions began to sprawl along the banks of the river.

Exploring by Car

Atlanta, unlike many other cities, has no natural boundaries. No ocean at its doorstep, no river to divide or mountains to ring the city. Because of this, the metropolitan area sprawls in almost all directions. In less than 20 years, Atlanta has grown from a small city to an enormous metropolitan area that is home to more than 3.5 million residents in 20 counties.

Driving in Atlanta is not simple. It is complicated, frustrating, and sometimes exhilarating. Atlanta is a curious mix of suburban developments and small in-town neighborhoods connected by winding tree-lined streets. Do not venture out without a good map, or you will soon be creating your own "how I got lost in Atlanta" tale.

Major Routes

To see some of the outlying areas and attractions surrounding Atlanta, it may be necessary or preferable to drive. Following is a list of the major routes in Atlanta and when you can expect the heaviest traffic.

- **I-285** (the Perimeter) circles the Metro Atlanta area.

- **I-85** runs northeast and southwest, continuing through South Carolina and Alabama.

- **I-75** runs northwest and southeast, continuing through Tennessee and Florida.

- **I-20** runs east and west, continuing through Alabama and South Carolina.

- **GA 400** runs from Buckhead to Dahlonega in the north.

Scenic Drives

Driving in Atlanta can be confusing, with it's profusion of Peachtree-something streets. But if you venture off the main streets you will be rewarded with drives along quiet, undulating roads that sweep through tree lined neighborhoods.

Jackson Street Bridge – A favorite of photographers and TV cameramen. If you've seen a panoramic shot of the city, it's likely it was taken from this location. From Downtown, take North Avenue east to Parkway Drive. Turn right and follow Parkway a few blocks until it turns into Jackson Street. The bridge is in the first block of Jackson Street. Make sure to visit this location during the day, as it is not safe after dark.

Exit #29 Bridge – Driving south on I-85, take Exit #29, also marked as GA 13 South (Peach Street). This bridge climbs up and down quickly, giving you a roller coaster view of the city. The buildings you see in the distance to the far right are those surrounding Lenox Square.

What locals call "the connector" is a seven-mile section of interstate through the middle of the city where I-75 and I-85 merge, "connecting" the north and south sides of town.

Along the Connector – Driving south along the connector between Martin Luther King, Jr. Boulevard and Ralph McGill Boulevard, there's an excellent view of the skyline.

From Lindbergh – From Peachtree Street, take Lindbergh Avenue east, to the intersection of Piedmont Avenue. Turn left on Piedmont, then immediately left again on Lindbergh (this section of Lindbergh is divided). Park free at the MARTA station and take time to linger and enjoy the view.

> ⊚ **TIP**
>
> An Atlanta pastime is locating a spectacular skyline view. Due in part to the hilly nature of the terrain in this part of north-central Georgia, the Atlanta skyline has a way of astonishing you at unexpected moments.

RUSH HOUR HEADACHES

Morning:

- ◎ **GA 400** southbound from 6:30-9
- ◎ **I-285** westbound from 7-8:30
- ◎ **I-85** southbound from 7-8:30
- ◎ **I-75** southbound from 6-9
- ◎ **I-20** westbound into the city from 7-8:30
- ◎ **I-20** eastbound into the city from 7-8:30

Afternoon:

- ◎ **GA 400** northbound from 4-7
- ◎ **I-285** rastbound from 330-6:30
- ◎ **I-85** northbound from 4-7
- ◎ **I-75** northbound from 4-7
- ◎ **I-20** from 4-6

Information Sources

In Atlanta

**THE ATLANTA CONVENTION
& VISITORS BUREAU**
233 Peachtree Street NE, Suite 100
Atlanta, GA 30303
☎ 404-521-6688
www.atlanta.com; e-mail acvb@atlanta.com

For information on attractions, hotels, conventions and a whole lot more. The Atlanta Convention &

Visitors Bureau can also supply you with maps and brochures for most of the major sights and forthcoming events and festivals. Don't forget to ask for their EXPLOR-A-CARD, which offers discounts on selected attractions, hotels, restaurants and shops.

VISITORS BUREAU LOCATIONS

- ◎ **Hartsfield Atlanta International Airport**, at the head of the escalator from the passenger concourses in the North and South baggage claim areas, open Mondays-Fridays, 9-9; Saturdays, noon-6 pm; Sundays 12:30-6 pm.

- ◎ **Underground Atlanta**, on the upper level, at the corner of Upper Alabama Street and Pryor, next to Heritage Row, open daily, noon-6 pm.

- ◎ **Lenox Square**, in the Concierge's booth near the main Peachtree Street entrance, open Tuesdays-Sundays, noon-6 pm.

- ◎ **Peachtree Center**, in the food court near the elevators. This location, open Mondays-Fridays, 8:30-5:30, is operated by the Peachtree Merchants Association; the information is the same as that available from the Atlanta Convention & Visitors Bureau outlets.

THE ATLANTA CHAMBER OF COMMERCE
235 International Boulevard NW
Atlanta, GA 30303
☎ 404-880-9000

The Chamber of Commerce provides information on business statistics and population growth, relocation, and employment.

GEORGIA DEPARTMENT OF INDUSTRY, TRADE, AND TOURISM
PO Box 1776
Atlanta, GA 30301
☎ 800-847-4842, www.georgia.org.

This agency is an excellent source for information on Atlanta and areas beyond the Perimeter. Be sure to contact them and ask for *Georgia On My Mind*, a publication that includes over 100 pages listing attractions, side trips, accommodations, and state parks.

Outside Atlanta

The following organizations can provide information to help you plan excursions outside of Atlanta:

Acworth Area Visitor Information Caboose, ☎ 770-974-7626

Albany Convention & Visitors Bureau, ☎ 404-883-6900

Atlanta's DeKalb Convention & Visitors Bureau, ☎ 404-378-2525

Clayton County Convention & Visitors Bureau, ☎ 770-478-4800

Cobb County Convention & Visitors Bureau, ☎ 678-303-COBB (2622)

Covington Convention & Visitors Bureau, ☎ 770-787-3868

Dahlonega/Lumpkin County Chamber of Commerce, ☎ 800-231-5543, 706-864-3711

Dalton Convention & Visitors Bureau, ☎ 706-272-7676

Douglasville Convention & Visitors Bureau, ☎ 770-947-5920

Gwinnett Convention & Visitors Bureau, ☎ 770-277-6212

Macon Bibb County Convention & Visitors Bureau, ☎ 912-743-3401

North Fulton Chamber of Commerce, ☎ 770-993-8806

Roswell Convention & Visitors Bureau, ☎ 770-640-3253

Sunup to Sundown

Almost everyone has an idea about what makes Atlanta an attractive destination. It could be a fascination with *Gone With The Wind* or a desire to celebrate the African-American experience. For some, it's a sportsman's paradise with major teams and events. Or, it could be a learning experience at one of many museums and cultural facilities.

Atlanta is one great cauldron of contradictions. It was the first major American city to elect a Black mayor, yet, until early 2001, the Georgia flag flying above the State Capitol, within sight of his office, still bore the Confederate emblem. It's a city that scurries for cover when a single flake of snow flurries to the ground, yet it has enthusiastically embraced a new professional hockey team.

It is a city that clings to its historic traditions while simultaneously pursuing all that is new and modern. With one foot firmly entrenched in its past and the other stepping boldly into a new millennium, Atlanta has much to offer the visitor.

Top Attractions

You'll have difficulty defining a singular "Atlanta" landmark or attraction. It is the romance of the Old South and the high speed pace of a NASCAR race. It is high-rise towers and antebellum mansions. Atlanta is many things to many visitors. It's a sports town, a convention city, a business center and a shopper's paradise. It is the epicenter of one of the most important social revolutions of the 20th century and the site of a historic battle. The contradictions are what make Atlanta unique among Southern cities.

Within its acclaimed museums, almost unending opportunities to shop, scenic wonders, and historic sites, you'll discover the secret of what makes Atlanta so impossible to stereotype.

There are walking tours of many of Atlanta's historic neighborhoods and outlying communities. Contact the Atlanta Preservation Center (see page 76) for information.

Downtown & Vicinity

ATLANTA CYCLORAMA
☎ 404-658-7625
Grant Park, 800 Cherokee Avenue SE
Hours: Tuesdays-Saturdays, 9:30-4:30, closed Thanksgiving, Christmas, New Year's Day, and Dr. Martin Luther King, Jr. Day.
Admission: $5 adults, $4 seniors, $3 children six-12
MARTA: Bus #31 from Five Points Station

The Cyclorama's The Battle of Atlanta is the world's largest painting.

Since 1898, Cyclorama's painting, "The Battle of Atlanta," has told the story of the 1864 conflict through narration, music, art and sound effects. This most unusual exhibition of history is both charming and impacting. The huge, panoramic painting in the round, completed in 1885, is an icon of a bygone era. This type of amusement was immensely popular at the turn of the century and its existence today is a testament to Atlanta's commitment to preserve its history. Don't expect an entirely pro-South approach to the Battle of Atlanta at the Cyclorama presentation. The message is decidedly anti-war.

CENTENNIAL OLYMPIC PARK
Techwood Drive and International Drive
☎ 404-222-PARK (7275)
MARTA: Peachtree Center or OMNI Station

A legacy of the 1996 Olympic Games, the 21-acre park is the site of the Fountain of Rings, the world's largest fountain utilizing the Olympic ring symbol; a court of 23 national flags, and a commemorative brick pathway. Photographers will delight in the dramatic views of Atlanta's ever-blossoming skyline. Four fountain shows daily, at 12:30, 3:30, 6:30 and 9:00.

CNN CENTER
One CNN Center
☎ 404-827-1500 or 827-2300, or 800-410-4CNN
Hours: 9 am-6 pm
MARTA: OMNI Station

This center houses the global headquarters of Turner Broadcasting System, plus the studios and newsrooms for CNN's international networks. Be a part of CNN's *Talk Back Live*, a daily show originating from the open air forum within the CNN Center. Tickets to the show are free and on a first-come, first-serve basis. The Center also houses a movie theater, restaurants, bank, post office and specialty stores, including the Braves Clubhouse Store and The Turner Store.

★ **DID YOU KNOW?**

The escalator in the CNN Center is the longest freestanding escalator in the world, rising 160 feet, or approximately eight stories, in height.

CNN STUDIO TOUR
One CNN Center
☎ 404-827-2300 or 877-CNN-TOUR
Hours: Call for tour schedule information
Admission: $7 adults, $5 seniors, $4.50 children six-12; children under six are not permitted on the tour
MARTA: OMNI/Dome/GWCC Station

Visitors can sign up for a behind the scenes tour of the global headquarters of CNN & Turner Broadcasting. Tours run continuously and are available in 16 languages. Take the deluxe tour at $25 and you'll get an up-close-and-personal view of how the news is put together. For an additional fee you can even don a CNN logo jacket, sit behind a simulated CNN News desk and, using a teleprompter, pretend to deliver the news; you get to keep the videotape of your performance as a "newscaster."

FOX THEATRE
660 Peachtree Street NE
☎ 404-881-2100
MARTA: North Avenue Station

Listed on the National Register of Historic Places, this 1929 Moorish/Egyptian/Art Deco fantasy hosts a wide range of live performances, a summer movie series and year-round tours. This fanciful auditorium, built in 1929 as a combination movie palace and Masonic Hall, is an extravaganza of excesses that must be seen to be believed. The ceiling of the theater suggests a night under a Bedouin chieftain's tent beneath a clear desert sky. The 96 stars that twinkle above are 11-watt bulbs fixed above two inch crystals. Clouds, rain and other effects are produced by special projectors. The Fox at one time was a venue for the Atlanta performances of the touring Metropolitan Opera, and such operatic greats as Robert Merrill, Ezio Pinza, Roberta Peters and Anna Moffo have graced the stage. To get the complete story, take time to participate in one of the tours of the Fox conducted by the Atlanta Preservation Center.

GEORGIA STATE CAPITOL
200 Washington Street
☎ 404-656-2844
www.sos.state.ga.us/tours/
Hours: 8-5, Mondays-Fridays
Admission: Free
MARTA: Georgia State Station

The Georgia State Legislature meets for only 40 days a year (except for special sessions), beginning the second Monday in January, in the circa-1889 building. Topped by a brilliant dome sheathed in gold leaf, the capitol is also home to the Georgia Capitol Museum, where current exhibits include Georgia animals and wildlife. Many of the exhibits are in storage until restoration is completed in 2001. Guided tours are offered weekdays.

The gold leaf atop the Georgia State Capitol dome was mined in Dahlonega, site of the country's first gold rush.

KING PLOW ARTS CENTER
887 Marietta Street
☎ 404-875-1606

This facility is in a renovated factory that now houses a 150-seat theater.

MARTIN LUTHER KING, JR.
NATIONAL HISTORIC SITE
450 Auburn Avenue NE
☎ 404-331-5190
www.nps.gov/malu
Hours: Daily, 10-5
Admission: Free, but you must obtain a ticket from the National Park Service office
MARTA: King Memorial Station to Bus #99 North Avenue, or Five Points Station to Bus #3 Auburn Avenue

The 42-acre Martin Luther King, Jr. National Historic Site encompasses the King Center and the King Birth Home on Auburn Avenue. Within the Visitor Center you'll find exhibits about Dr. King, as well as information on other National Parks in the area and across the Southeast. The National Parks Service conducts tours of the King Birth Home every hour from 10 to 5 daily.

MARTIN LUTHER KING, JR. CENTER
FOR NONVIOLENT SOCIAL CHANGE
449 Auburn Avenue NE
☎ 404-526-8900
www.thekingcenter.com
Hours: 9-5 (6 pm during summer)
Admission: No charge to visit the Freedom Hall
MARTA: King Memorial Station to Bus #99, North
Avenue; or Five points Station to Bus #3, Auburn
Avenue.

The King Center is Atlanta's most visited attraction.
Every day visitors make their way past the eternal
flame in the center's plaza and toward the reflecting
pool. In the center of the pool stands Dr. King's ele-
vated marble tomb. The King Center's exhibition
hall contains a permanent display of memorabilia
and photographs of Dr. King's public and private
life. The center's library houses the world's largest
collection of first hand accounts of the Civil Rights
movement.

SCITREK
395 Piedmont Avenue
☎ 404-522-5500
www.scitrek.org
Hours: Daily, 10-5; closed on major holidays
Admission: $7.50 adults; $5 children, seniors, students and military personnel with identification
MARTA: Civic Center Station

If you have a budding Einstein or Madam Curie
within your family, this is the place to take him or
her for some hands-on experience. Interactive exhibits, a Cyber Playground, the Electromagnetic Junction and the Information Petting Zoo are just a few
of the experiences you'll discover within SciTrek.
This hands-on approach to science allows visitors to

explore math and technology in a way that is both interesting and lively.

Permanent exhibits include a 40-foot-tall lighted replica of the Eiffel Tower made of erector set pieces; an Electric Magnetic Junction that lets you close a circuit with your own body; and Mind's Eye, a perception and illusion exhibit that explores the range and limits of the human senses.

UNDERGROUND ATLANTA
Peachtree at Alabama Street
☎ 404-523-2311
Hours: Monday-Saturday, 10 am-9:30 pm; Sunday, 10 am-5 pm
MARTA: Five Points Station

Underground Atlanta is the site for the dropping of the "Big Peach" on New Year's Eve.

Built on the underpinnings of early Atlanta, this one-time railroad gulch is now a spirited urban marketplace, featuring restaurants, specialty shops, street vendors and entertainment emporiums, all underground. This is perfect for a rainy day, as you can even access the Underground directly from the MARTA station at Five Points. Unless you have been sequestered in a remote location, however, there is very little in Underground Atlanta that you cannot find at any other mall or tourist trap in the United States. The chain stores have overtaken this location.

SWEET AUBURN DISTRICT
MARTA: King Memorial Station to #99 North Avenue bus, or Five Points Station to the #3 Auburn Avenue bus.

Sweet Auburn is an area in downtown Atlanta along Auburn Avenue, running from Courtland Street east to Randolph Street. This National Historic District, the nucleus of Atlanta's African-American community, was the cradle of the civil rights movement. Martin Luther King, Jr., was born at 501 Auburn Avenue. His father and grandfather preached at Ebenezer Baptist Church, and nearby, the Martin Luther King, Jr., Center for Nonviolent Social Change enshrines his tomb.

WREN'S NEST
1050 Ralph Abernathy Blvd. SW
☎ 404-753-7735
Hours: Tuesday-Saturday, 10-4, Sunday, 1-4
Admission: $6 adults, $4 seniors and teens, $3 children four to 12
MARTA: West End Station to Bus #71 (Cascade)

Wren's Nest, in the West End section of Atlanta, was the home of Joel Chandler Harris, creator of the Uncle Remus stories, from 1881 to his death in 1908. This turn-of-the-century Queen Anne-style house is both a National Historic and City of Atlanta Landmark. Throughout the year, storytellers spin many of Harris' charming tales. Visitors also enjoy the guided tours and the museum shop filled with Br'er Rabbit books and memorabilia.

WORLD OF COCA-COLA
55 Martin Luther King, Jr. Drive
☎ 404-676-5151
Hours: Monday-Saturday, 9-5; Sunday, noon-6
Admission: $6 adults, $4 seniors 55+, $3 children under 12, under six free
MARTA: Five Points Station

This attraction features a three-story celebration, and sales pitch, of the soft drink known around the world. Take a self-guided tour and sample the taste of Coca-Cola along with soft drinks from over 40 countries. In the "Everything Coca-Cola" store you'll find a large selection of branded merchandise. The

The "hobble-skirt" Coca-Cola bottle design was borrowed from the Encyclopaedia Britannica's line drawing of a cola nut, which was defined as "a bulbous pod with longitudinal ridges."

1930s-era Barnes soda fountain comes complete with a jukebox and soda jerk on duty. *Every Day of Your Life* is a 10-minute celebration of life and Coca-Cola around the world. Yes, it's a big commercial, but Coca-Cola is an integral part of Atlanta and its financial success.

ZOO ATLANTA

As part of the American Zoo and Aquarium Association's Species Survival Plan, 11 endangered Western Lowland Gorillas have been born at Zoo Atlanta's Ford African Rain Forest since it opened in 1988.

Grant Park, 800 Cherokee Avenue SE
☎ 404-624-5600
www.zooatlanta.org
Hours: Monday-Sunday, 9:30-5
Admission: $15adults, $11seniors, $10 children ages three to 11
MARTA: #97 or #105 Bus from the Westend station

It's "Panda-monium!" Zoo Atlanta is one of the oldest zoos in the United States, and is home to nearly 1,000 animals living in naturalistic habitats, including African elephants, black rhinos, lions, tigers, red pandas and Sumatran orangutans. Recently, two giant pandas from the Peoples Republic of China have joined Atlanta's favorite menagerie.

Midtown

ATLANTA BOTANICAL GARDEN

The Atlanta Botanical Gardens gift shop is filled with unexpected delights for gardeners and non-gardeners alike.

Piedmont Park, 1345 Piedmont Avenue
☎ 404-876-5859
www.atlantabotanicalgarden.org
Hours: Tuesday-Sunday, 9 am-6 pm
Admission: $6 adults, $5 seniors, $3 children six-11; free Thursdays, 3 pm-close
MARTA: Midtown or Arts Center

This is where Atlanta takes time to stop and smell the roses. Tropical, desert and endangered plants from around the world are shown year-round in the

Fuqua Conservatory, just three miles from Downtown. The gardens are perched on the edge of Piedmont Park and contain more than 3,000 ornamental plants in the display gardens.

CENTER FOR PUPPETRY ARTS
1404 Spring Street
☎ 404-873-3089 (schedule) or 404-873-3391 (tickets)
www.puppet.org
Hours: Call for performance and workshop schedule
Admission: Adults, $8; students and seniors $7
MARTA: Arts Center Station

This center houses a museum and offers performances and create-a-puppet workshops for all age groups. The purpose of the center is to explore puppetry as an international, ancient and popular art form. Video of performances by Wayland Flowers and Madame are shown to exemplify the use of adult humor in puppetry. Madame herself is also on display, along with other adult puppets. The Center for Puppetry Arts is the only facility of its kind in the continental United States.

> ⊚ **TIP**
>
> Children ages five and older can participate in a "Create-A-Puppet" workshop where they will learn the art of puppetry by making their own puppets.

MARGARET MITCHELL HOUSE AND MUSEUM

999 Peachtree Street at 10th Street
☎ 404-249-7012
www.gwtw.org
Hours: Daily, 9-4
Admission: adults $10, seniors & students $9, children (under five) free
MARTA: Midtown Station

Gone With The Wind has sold more hardcover copies in the US than any book but the Bible.

Author Margaret Mitchell resided here from 1925 to 1932, during which time she wrote the epic novel *Gone With The Wind*, one of the most popular novels of the 20th century. Ms. Mitchell referred to her apartment (and all the other locations where she lived) as "the dump." This museum has struggled for existence. It was burned on at least three occasions. Prior to the 1996 Olympic Games, Daimler-Benz funded a complete restoration of the house as a museum.

The one-hour, docent-led tour includes a video of Mitchell's life, photographs and archival exhibits, as well as a visit to her apartment.

Buckhead

GOVERNOR'S MANSION

391 West Paces Ferry Road, NE
☎ 404-261-1776
Hours: 10-11:30 am, Tuesday, Wednesday, Thursday
Admission: free
MARTA: Bus #40 (West Paces Ferry) from Lindbergh Center Station

The Governor's Mansion is a gem of a Greek Revival-style building. Thirty rooms are furnished with early 19th-century American paintings and porcelain, and a remarkable collection of Federal-period furniture. Visitors can take a self-guided tour Tuesdays through Thursdays. The Atlanta History Center (see page 80) is located one mile west of the Governor's Mansion.

Druid Hills

FERNBANK MUSEUM OF NATURAL HISTORY
767 Clifton Road, NE
☎ 404-370-0960
Hours: Open Mondays-Saturdays, 10-5; Sundays, 12-5
MARTA: #2 Bus to Clifton Road

Take in an IMAX Theater presentation and a "Walk Through Time in Georgia." The museum is visually dazzling with its dramatic, 86-foot-high Great Hall Skylight and spectacular wall of windows. Even the flooring of fossil-embedded limestone will amaze. Exhibits at the Fernbank include "The World of Shells," a spectacular collection of exotic shells and mollusks from the Georgia coastline and from around the world, and "Cultures of the World," a collection of jewelry, costumes and textiles from ancient Persia, Tibet and other exotic locations.

FERNBANK SCIENCE CENTER
156 Heaton Park Drive NE
☎ 404-378-4311
www.fernbank.edu
Hours: Mondays, 8:30-5; Tuesdays-Fridays, 8:30 am-10 pm; Saturdays, 10-5; Sundays, 1-5 pm.
Admission: Planetarium shows are $2 for adults, $1 for children; general admission is free.
MARTA: #2 Bus to Clifton Road

This intriguing attraction, about a mile from the Fernbank Museum of Natural History (see above), is owned and funded by the DeKalb County school system. It is home to one of the largest planetariums in the United States, and the exhibit hall houses an original Apollo capsule, authentic moon rock, and much more space memorabilia. Come on a clear Friday evening and join the astronomer on duty for a tour of the galaxy through the observatory's telescope.

Little Five Points

CARTER PRESIDENTIAL CENTER, LIBRARY AND MUSEUM
453 Freedom Parkway
☎ 404-331-3942
Hours: Monday-Saturday, 9-4:45, closed Thanksgiving, Christmas and New Year's day
Admission: $5 adults, $3 seniors, 16 & under free
MARTA: From Five Points Station take Bus #16

The only Presidential library in the southeastern United States examines and honors the early life, political career and presidency of Jimmy Carter. On permanent display in the Carter Museum are hundreds of artifacts from his years in the White House (1977-1980), including the Camp David Accords. A special exhibit, "Impressions of a White House Christmas," features a recreation of the Carter tree, circa 1980. Lovely gardens, great view of Atlanta's skyline and a gift shop with unusual souvenirs complete the experience.

Decatur & Surrounding Area

STONE MOUNTAIN PARK
Highway 78, PO Box 778
Village of Stone Mountain, GA, 30086
☎ 770-498-5690, www.stonemountainpark.com
Hours: Year-round, 6 am to midnight; attraction hours vary
Admission: $16 for adults; $13 ages three-11; parking $6
MARTA: #120 Stone Mountain bus from Avondale Station, transfer to #19 bus

The world's largest granite monolith, just 16 miles east of downtown Atlanta, Stone Mountain rises 825 feet above a 3,200-acre lake. The park also features a scenic railroad, an antebellum plantation, a natural habitat zoo and petting farm, and an antique auto and music museum. On the mountain's north face is the world's largest bas-relief carving, featuring the likenesses of Confederate President Jefferson Davis, General Robert E. Lee and General "Stonewall" Jackson. On Easter Sunday, an interdenominational service is held at sunrise. The view from the summit is worth the trek.

Museums

Atlanta's compendium of museums is astonishing in variety and scope. The fine arts, folk arts, African-American arts as well as the struggle for civil rights and the Civil War are all amply represented. Considering that Atlanta is barely more than 150 years old, the dramas it has experienced, and the array of cultural activities, are amazing.

Downtown & Vicinity

ATLANTA CONTEMPORARY ART CENTER
535 Means Street
☎ 404-688-1970
Hours: Tuesday through Saturday, 11 am-5 pm
Admission: Adults $3, Students and Seniors $1
MARTA: from Five Points station take the #1 bus to
Marietta and Means Streets

The center, located northwest of Centennial Olympic Park off Marietta Street, hosts a wide range of contemporary art and visual rhythm presentations. The 40,000-square-foot center houses an art book press, studios, a large gallery that presents major exhibitions, and a performance café.

THE APEX (AFRICAN-AMERICAN PANORAMIC EXPERIENCE) MUSEUM
135 Auburn Avenue, NE
☎ 404-523-2739
Hours: Tuesday-Saturday, 10-5
Admission: $3 adults, $2 students/senior citizens
MARTA: from Five Points Station, take #3 Auburn
Avenue bus to Piedmont Avenue.

The museum is currently housed in a small building adjacent to the Auburn Avenue Research Library. Plans eventually call for it to have its own specially designed, 97,00- square-foot facility. This location includes a replica of an Atlanta streetcar, in which visitors sit to watch a film that tells the story of the Auburn Avenue neighborhood. Exhibits include African and slavery-era artifacts, and a re-creation of a Black-owned drug store on Auburn Avenue.

ATLANTA INTERNATIONAL MUSEUM OF ART AND DESIGN
285 Peachtree Avenue
Peachtree Center, Marquis Two
☎ 404-688-2467
Hours: Monday-Friday, 11-5
Admission: Free
MARTA: Peachtree Center

Atlanta's only exclusively international museum, focusing on international cultural understanding through exhibits and educational programs.

IVAN ALLEN, JR.
BRAVES MUSEUM & HALL OF FAME
Turner Field, 755 Hank Aaron Drive
☎ 404-614-2310
Hours: Vary with the seasons, call for times
Museum Admission: $7 for adults, $4 for children. Special note: Admission to the Museum is $2 on game days with a ticket to the ball game.
MARTA: Shuttle buses run from Five Points station on game days.

The museum, on the Terrace Level at Turner Field, traces the Braves history from their beginnings in Boston, through their years in Milwaukee, and finally to Atlanta. It's open year-round, and houses over 200 pieces of baseball memorabilia, including the bat Hank Aaron used to hit his record-breaking 715th home run. The museum is run by the Atlanta History Center, which treats the Braves Museum as a serious historical subject, never forgetting that baseball is a wonderful, spirited game.

Sunup to Sundown

HAMMONDS HOUSE
503 Peeples Street
☎ 404-752-8730
Hours: Tuesdays-Fridays, 10-6; Saturdays-Sundays, 1-5 pm
Admission: $2 adults, $1 children, students and seniors
MARTA: #71 bus from West End Station

The Hammonds House Galleries and Resource Center of African-American Art showcases Haitian and African-American art, through permanent and changing exhibitions. The O.T. Hammonds Collection features works by painter and collagist Romare Bearden, and some of the best contemporary African-American art from Atlanta and around the country.

HERNDON HOME
587 University Place NW
☎ 404-581-9813
Hours: Tuesdays-Saturdays, 10-3
Admission: Free, but donations are accepted
Tours: Start at the top of each hour, cost is $3.50.
MARTA: Vine City Station

Built in 1910, this Beaux-Arts classical mansion in close proximity to Atlanta University is as amazing as the man who built it. Alonzo Herndon began life as a slave, and had little formal education; he was later trained as a barber. Eventually his barber shop employed 40 men, and he founded the Atlanta Life Insurance Company. Alonzo Herndon became one of the wealthiest men in Atlanta. The house is outfitted opulently, with nine fireplaces, a mahogany dining room, and even a mural that tells the story of his rise from slavehood to entrepreneur.

HIGH MUSEUM OF ART FOLK ART & PHOTOGRAPHY GALLERIES

Georgia-Pacific Building
30 John Wesley Dobbs Ave.
☎ 404-577-6940
Hours: Mondays-Saturdays, 10-5; closed Sundays
Admission: Donation is requested
MARTA: Peachtree Center Station

Located in the heart of Atlanta's business and convention district, this is one of the largest branch museums in the country. The Downtown satellite facility of the High Museum of Art offers a continuous program of changing exhibitions, featuring folk art and photography.

Sumup to Sundown

⊚ TIP

Walk a short distance from the Georgia-Pacific Building to the **Candler Building**, at the corner of Peachtree Street and John Wesley Dobbs Avenue, and discover the likenesses of Raphael, Shakespeare, Buffalo Bill Cody, Cyrus McCormick, Georgia writers Joel Chandler Harris and Sidney Lanier, as well as Asa Candler's parents, carved in marble on the exterior.

MARTIN LUTHER KING, JR.
NATIONAL HISTORIC SITE
450 Auburn Avenue NE
☎ 404-331-6922
www.nps.org/malu
Hours: Daily, 9-5
Admission: Free
MARTA: King Memorial station to #99 bus, or Five
Points station to #3 bus.

Relive the dream at the birthplace and home of Dr.
Martin Luther King, Jr. In the Visitor Center, you'll
experience an emotional exhibit of the civil rights
struggle. Follow with a visit to the birth home of
young Martin, then move onto the Ebenezer Baptist
Church, where you may view King family artifacts
and a Gandhi exhibition in Freedom Hall. All activities are free.

Midtown

ATLANTA PRESERVATION CENTER
156 Seventh St. NE, Suite #3
☎ 404-876-2040

Not exactly a museum, the APC is a non-profit mem-
bership organization that promotes the preservation of Atlanta's historically, architecturally and
culturally significant buildings, neighborhoods and
districts. The Preservation Center's walking tours of
many of Atlanta's established neighborhoods and favorite attractions are a delight for visitors of all
ages. The Atlanta Preservation Center turns Atlanta's streets and landmarks into an open-air museum
to be strolled and sauntered through.

HIGH MUSEUM OF ART
1280 Peachtree Street NE
☎ 404-733-4400
Hours: Tues.-Sat., 10-5; Sun., noon-5;
closed Mondays and holidays
Admission: $6; $4 seniors and college students; $2
children ages six-17; free for Museum members and
children under six
MARTA: Arts Center Station

Founded in 1905 as the Atlanta Art Association, the
High Museum of Art today ranks as Atlanta's premier venue for the visual arts. Its 135,000-square
foot-facility is the award-winning work of architect
Richard Meier. This beautiful, modern building
houses fine collections of European and American
paintings and sculpture, African, decorative, and
20th-century art, photography and graphics. Recent
exhibitions have included a Norman Rockwell retro-
spective; John Twactman: An American Impressionist; and Narrative of African-American Art of the
20th Century.

MARGARET MITCHELL HOUSE
& GONE WITH THE WIND MUSEUM
990 Peachtree Street
☎ 404-249-7015
www.gwtw.org
Hours: Daily, 9-4
Admission: $7 adults, $6 seniors, students, youth
seven-17, children under five free
MARTA: Midtown Station or Bus #10

Margaret Mitchell House

Tour the historic building and apartment where
Margaret Mitchell wrote one of the world's most be-
loved novels, *Gone With The Wind*, and learn about
the life of this fascinating woman. Mitchell and her
husband lived in a tiny, dark apartment, which to-

day contains the original typewriter she used to transcribe the novel from her handwritten manuscript (quite a task at over 1,000 pages), and her 1937 Pulitzer Prize.

Peggy, as she was known, and her husband, John Marsh, were a fun-loving couple, and their Peachtree Street apartment became a gathering place for Bohemian Atlanta. In their memory the Bohemian Club was created, and now meets the third Wednesday of every month, 7-9:30 pm, at the Margaret Mitchell Museum. A donation of $7 is requested.

Gone With The Wind Museum

The original manuscript of Gone With the Wind *filled 60 manila envelopes when completed.*

Opened in late 1999, the museum is filled with exhibits and artifacts illuminating the making of the movie, its premiere, and its legacy. Some of the major acquisitions include the front door of the legendary Tara plantation from the movie set, and the portrait of Scarlett that hung over the mantel of the Butler home. Other artifacts in the museum include the world's largest collection of *Gone With The Wind* memorabilia, such as dolls, games, plates and jewelry, owned by collector Herb Bridges. Film footage from the premiere and original set design sketches, props, and scripts are also found here.

★ **DID YOU KNOW?**

Gone With The Wind grossed $14 million in its first year alone, and received a record 10 Academy Awards, including the first ever for a black actress. When the movie aired for the first time on television in 1976, 110 million people tuned in to watch.

RHODES HALL
1516 Peachtree Street NW
☎ 404-885-7800
Hours: weekdays 11 am-4 pm, Sundays, noon-3 pm, closed Saturdays
MARTA: Arts Center Station or Bus #23

Created in the style of a Rhineland castle, this Romanesque Revival-style mansion is one you won't want to miss. Built at the turn of the century for furniture magnate Amos Rhodes, the house features exquisite stained-glass windows and an elaborately carved mahogany staircase.

THE WILLIAM BREMAN
JEWISH HERITAGE MUSEUM
1440 Spring Street NW
☎ 404-873-1661
Hours: Monday-Thursday, 10-5; Friday, 10-3; Sunday, 1-5
Admission: $5 adults, $3 seniors and students, children under six free
MARTA: Arts Center Station

The largest Museum of its kind in the Southeast is located in the heart of Atlanta's business and convention district. Atlanta's Jewish Heritage and the Holocaust are featured. The museum, in the neighborhood of the High Museum, the Center for Puppetry Arts and Rhodes Hall, also contains a library, archives, and museum shop.

Buckhead

ATLANTA HISTORY CENTER
130 West Paces Ferry Road, NW
☎ 404-814-4000
www.atlantahistory.net
Hours: Monday-Saturday, 10-5:30; Sunday, noon-5:30 pm
Admission: $10 adults, $8 students and seniors; $4 youths six-17, children under five free
MARTA: #23 bus to West Paces Ferry Road, walk west past the second traffic light (Slaton Drive) to the pedestrian entrance.

From cotton fields to railroads, the Civil War to civil rights, you'll discover the true story of Atlanta's past. Set on 33 acres of woods and gardens in the Buckhead district, the history center includes a permanent museum as well as an 1840s farmstead, the Tullie Smith Farm, and a 1920s in-town mansion, the Swan House. Permanent exhibits at the Atlanta History Center include "Turning Point: The American Civil War," "In Scarlett's Footsteps," and the Dubose Civil War Collection. The showpiece of the Atlanta History Center is the Swan House, built in 1928 by Philip Trammell Shutze, one of the greatest classical architects of the 20th century. The Center also features a Museum Shop, The Coca-Cola Café, Swan Coach House restaurant, and a picnic area.

Druid Hills

CALLANWOLDE FINE ARTS CENTER
980 Briarcliff Road NE
☎ 404-872-5338
www.callanwolde.org
Hours: Monday-Friday, 9-9; Saturday, 9-2
Admission: free; call for event schedule
MARTA: from Lindbergh station take the #48 bus

Callanwolde, in Druid Hills, is a unique institution. This magnificent, Gothic Tudor-style mansion, built in the 1920s for Charles Howard Candler (son of Coca-Cola founder Asa Griggs Candler), is listed on the National Register of Historic Places. Callanwolde hosts art exhibits, concerts, recitals and dramatic presentations. Christmas at Callanwolde is an Atlanta tradition (see page 25); the mansion is decked with exquisite furnishings, majestic trees and sparkling lights. The house is surrounded by 12 acres of sculptured lawn and formal gardens. No guided tours are offered, but Callanwolde hosts arts programs throughout the year and is also available for private functions.

FERNBANK MUSEUM OF NATURAL HISTORY
767 Clifton Road NE
☎ 404-370-0730, www.fernbank.edu
Hours: Mondays-Saturdays, 10-5; Sundays 12-5
Admission: $8.95 adults, $7.95 seniors, $6.95 children three -12
MARTA: #2 Bus to Clifton Road

This is the largest natural history museum in the Southeast, and boasts Georgia's first IMAX theater. Permanent installations include "Walk Through Time in Georgia," 17 galleries with exhibits that explore land formations within the state and the chronological development of life on earth; the Dinosaur Hall, featuring seven life-size dinosaur models, and dramatic murals of the Cretaceous, Jurassic and Triassic eras; and the Okefenokee Swamp Gallery, which surrounds you with the sights and sounds of the strange and rare beauty of the swamp. The museum is visually dazzling with its dramatic, 86-foot-high Great Hall Skylight and spectacular wall of windows. Even the flooring of fossil-embedded limestone will amaze.

Decatur

MICHAEL C. CARLOS MUSEUM
EMORY UNIVERSITY
571 S. Kilgo Street, Decatur
☎ 404-727-4282
www.cc.emory.edu/CARLOS
Hours: Monday-Saturday, 10-5; Sunday, noon-5 pm
Admission: $3 donation suggested
MARTA: from Arts Center Station take the #36 bus; get off at the intersection of S. Kilgo Circle and N. Decatur Road

The museum features a permanent collection of approximately 18,000 objects, including art from Egypt, Greece, Italy, the Near East, the Americas, Asia, and Oceania, and artworks on paper ranging from the Middle Ages to the 20th century. The museum also offers special exhibitions from its own holdings and from other institutions, both national and international, and occupies a 45,000-square-foot building designed by architect Michael Graves.

Outside Atlanta

KENNESAW MOUNTAIN
CIVIL WAR MUSEUM
2829 Cherokee Street NW
☎ 770-427-2117
Kennesaw, GA

This museum is part of the Kennesaw Mountain National Battlefield Park. It incorporates exhibits relating to the Battle of Kennesaw Moutain, including "The General," a steam locomotive used in the Disney film *The Great Locomotive Chase*. The events in the film are based on the 1862 battle.

From downtown Atlanta, go north on I-75 to Exit 273; turn left on Wade-Green Road (which changes its name to Cherokee Street after you cross the freeway). The museum is on the right, approximately 2½ miles from the exit. Look for the red caboose.

Parks

In Atlanta you won't have to search very far to meet the challenge of the great outdoors. Atlanta has long been known as a city of trees, a city set within a forest. An organization, **Trees of Atlanta**, is entirely dedicated to keeping the city green. So, go ahead, lace on some athletic shoes, choose your venue and get moving! The Atlanta Parks Department information number is ☎ 404-817-6744.

Feeling fleet of foot? Popular running spots in the city include **Piedmont** and **Grant parks**. Both have miles of enticing trails.

Pedal pushers should head for **Piedmont Park** or **Stone Mountain Park**. Bike rentals are available adjacent to both locations.

Ready to take a hike? Just a short distance outside the city you can revel in the trails of **Stone Mountain Park**, **Amicalola Falls** or the **Chattahoochee National Forest**.

If you just want to paddle your own canoe, the **Chattahoochee Outdoor Center**, just 30 minutes from Downtown (see page 102 for details), has rentals of both rafts and canoes.

Downtown & Vicinity

CENTENNIAL PARK
Marietta Street and Techwood Drive
MARTA: OMNI/Dome/GWCC

This was the city's best souvenir of the 1996 Olympic Games. The park was privately funded for the Olympic Games, and now belongs to the state. It is the largest center-city park developed in the United States within the last 20 years. (That's Atlanta! Don't just build any park, make it the largest.) The distinctive light towers, fountains and commemorative brick walks, and very popular Fountain of Rings, are special legacies left behind from the 1996 Olympic Games. The Fountain of Rings is the world's largest fountain utilizing the Olympic symbol of five connecting rings; it features 25 jets of water. Try to catch one of the four 20-minute water shows each day, at 12:30, 3:30, 6:30 and 9:00. Other features in the park include a court of 24 flags, a natural amphitheater seating 1,200, and a six-acre great lawn. The park hosts many activities; one of the liveliest is the Fourth of July fireworks celebration. This is a terrific place to bring your children if they need to run off some energy after a day of museums or shopping.

GRANT PARK
Georgia and Cherokees Avenues SE
MARTA: Bus #31 from Lindbergh or Five Points stations

Historic Grant Park is about two miles south of Downtown. Loaded with history, Grant Park was once home to the Creek Indians, and in later years was lined with Confederate artillery troops during the Battle of Atlanta. Grant Park is most noted for Zoo Atlanta and the Atlanta Cyclorama, but you will also find athletic fields for football and softball.

Midtown

PIEDMONT PARK
Piedmont Avenue and 14th Street
☎ 404-817-6744
MARTA: Arts Center Station, Bus #36

Piedmont Park is the city's largest, with tennis courts, a swimming pool, softball fields, playgrounds, and paved trails for jogging, hiking, biking, and skating. In summer you'll find it filled with sun-tanning bodies. The brave of heart can rent in-line skates and roller skates at **Skate Escape**, across from the park at 1086 Piedmont Avenue, ☎ 404-892-1292. Wait until you cross the street to put on your skates; the traffic on Piedmont Avenue can be unforgiving. The park is home to many festivals, fairs and symphony concerts throughout the year. In 1895 the Cotton States and International Exposition took place in Piedmont Park, and much of the park's current configuration dates from this event. The Peace Monument Arch at the 14th Street entrance to the park

The 1895 Exposition at Piedmont Park drew close to a million visitors during its three-month duration. John Philip Sousa's band premiered the King Cotton March, written expressly for the event.

was built in 1904 to signify the growing reconciliation between the North and South. It is said that most of the funds collected came from the North.

Buckhead

CHASTAIN PARK
235 W. Wieuca Road
☎ 404 817-6744
MARTA: #36 Chastain Bus from Lindbergh Station

Many Atlantans pack an elegant picnic supper for concerts at Chastain Park, complete with candles, wine and linen.

Located approximately eight miles north of Downtown between Lake Forrest Drive and Powers Ferry Road, Chastain Park has provided a respite from the hustle and bustle of city life for more than 40 years. It's famous for its amphitheater, which seats more than 6,000 and draws entertainers from a wide range of disciplines. In summer you'll find everything from the Atlanta Symphony to the Kingston Trio onstage at Chastain. Within Chastain Park is a 3½-mile jogging trail, athletic fields for baseball, softball, soccer and football, picnic and playground areas, and a swimming pool.

CHATTAHOOCHEE RIVER NATIONAL RECREATION AREA
Headquarters
1978 Island Ford Pkwy
Dunwoody, GA
☎ 770-399-8070

Raft "down the hooch," wander its hiking trails or just play in the playgrounds (but whatever you do, DO NOT drink the water; it is highly polluted). The Recreational Area, managed by the National Park Service, consists of 16 separate land units along a 48-mile stretch of the Chattahoochee River, north and northeast of Atlanta. Facilities are open from dawn to dusk, and include areas for fishing, hiking, rafting, canoeing, and picnicking. The parks also contain natural habitiats, nineteenth century historic sites, and Native American archeological sites.

To reach the headquarters and the Island Ford site, which is about 20 miles north of downtown Atlanta, go north on I-85 to Exit 87, onto Hwy 400 north. Take Exit 6 to Northridge Road going west, then take the first right onto Dunwoody Place. Turn right onto Roberts Drive, and right again onto Island Ford Parkway.

Atlanta's Heritage

Desperately Seeking Scarlett

Moonlight, magnolias, hoop skirts, and the torrid affair between Scarlett and Rhett are firmly entrenched images of what makes Atlanta, Atlanta. Every year visitors come to the city desperately seeking Tara, Twelve Oaks and all those other magical and mythical places Margaret Mitchell created.

Begin your search for Scarlett at the **Margaret Mitchell House** at 990 Peachtree Street (see pages 68 and 77). It was in this small apartment, while recuperating from an ankle injury, that Mitchell composed her lengthy opus. Within these tiny, dark rooms remains the original typewriter on which she transcribed her handwritten notes.

Daimler-Benz restored Margaret Mitchell's home on Peachtree Street for the Olympic celebrations.

Margaret Mitchell, known to family and friends as Peggy, claimed that Scarlett was based on her domineering grandmother, Annie Fitzgerald Stephens.

Sunup to Sundown

She often visited her grandparents, who lived south of Atlanta, in the Jonesboro area, near Folsom and Tara Roads. The stories of the Civil War were told and retold to Peggy, and it was from these memorable tales of courage and endurance that *Gone With The Wind* took seed.

To visit Jonesboro, drive south on I-75; take Exit 233, then turn right onto Jonesboro Road (which changes its name to Main Street when you enter the town). Jonesboro is approximately 18 miles from Atlanta. Almost the entire downtown area of Jonesboro appears much as it did before the Civil War; although the town was set afire, the brick exteriors of the buildings withstood the blaze. Start with a visit to the Jonesboro Depot Welcome Center at 104 N. Main Street.

While at the welcome center make sure you stop at the "Road To Tara" Museum, which houses one of the largest permanent collections of *Gone With The Wind* memorabilia.

◎ TIP

Historical and Hysterical Tours, ☎ 770-478-4800, operated by historian Pete Bonner, offer a treasure trove of trivia about Margaret Mitchell and *Gone With the Wind*.

While in Jonesboro take time to tour the **Stately Oaks Plantation**, 100 Carriage Lane at Jodeco Road, ☎ 770-473-0197. This plantation home was one of the inspirations for Mitchell's work. It was also a landmark for both Confederate and Union troops, who camped in the fields around the house during the Battle of Jonesboro. The Plantation is open Mondays-Saturdays, 10:30-3:30; however, it is a favorite site for weddings on Saturdays, so it is best to call ahead to make sure you will be able to tour. Admission is $6 for adults, $5 for seniors, and $3 for children.

Ashley Oaks at 144 College Street, ☎ 770-478-8986, a red brick mansion with graceful verandas, was another of Mitchell's inspirations for *Gone With the Wind*. Built from more than one million handmade bricks, and surrounded by ancient trees, it's a salute to a bygone era. Ashley Oaks is open Tuesdays-Saturdays, 12-3. If you are visiting in December, call ahead, as the house is often used for holiday parties. Admission is $5 for adults and $3 for children.

Back in Atlanta you'll want to be certain to visit the site of the premiere of *Gone With The Wind*. The pink granite **Georgia-Pacific** headquarters, at the intersection of Peachtree and Forsyth Streets, was built on the site of Loews Grand Theatre, where *Gone With the Wind* opened on December 15, 1939. The movie was also shown here in 1947, 1954, 1961 and 1967. The theater was destroyed by fire in 1979; there is an inscription on the wall to the right of the main entrance to the Georgia-Pacific building.

Many people mistakenly think that the Fox Theatre, at 660 Peachtree Street NE, was the site of the premiere of *Gone With the Wind*. This is partly because when Ted Turner aquired the rights to the film in 1989, he celebrated the 50th anniversary of the movie's release with a special showing of the restored film at the Fox. The theater is also across the street from **The Georgian Terrace Hotel** (659 Peachtree Street, ☎ 404-897-1911), where the film's stars stayed in 1939. Today, much of the hotel's grandeur remains intact (see page 150).

Tragically, in 1949 Margaret Mitchell was struck by
an automobile near Peachtree and 13th Streets. She
died from brain damage five days later, and was bur-
ied in Oakland Cemetery, in downtown Atlanta at
248 Oakland Avenue. Margaret Mitchell's grave is
Oakland Cemetery's most frequently visited site.
The author shares a simple headstone with her husband, so look for the name Marsh rather than Mitchell. The plot is carefully tended and, in a Southern
burial custom, cedars are planted at the four corners.

The Battle of Atlanta

Atlanta figured prominently in the Civil War, and
the loss of the city sealed the South's doom. What is
most commonly referred to as the Battle of Atlanta
was actually a series of battles, conducted from June
to September of 1864, a fierce struggle ranging from
Decatur to Atlanta for control of the railway. These
are the episodes depicted in the painting at the
Cyclorama (see page 58). Some of the most intense
fighting took place in what is now the parking lot of
the Inman Park/Reynoldstown MARTA station.

Union forces slowly encircled the city like a noose,
and then squeezed it shut. The first clash was at
Kennesaw Mountain, just north of the city, then
came Peachtree Creek; next was Decatur, then Ezra
Church and finally Jonesboro.

> ## ⊚ *TIP*
>
> Seeing the sights of the Confederacy can take you all over the Atlanta metro area. For a short tour, you might want to first visit the Cyclorama in Grant Park, just south of Downtown; then go to Oakland Cemetery, the final resting place of hundreds of Civil War soldiers; and end your tour at Kennesaw Mountain National Battlefield Park.

Kennesaw Mountain

Kennesaw Mountain National Battlefield Park, northwest of Marietta off I-75 (Kennesaw Mountain Drive, Kennesaw, GA, ☎ 770-427-4686), is the site of a pivotal battle fought in June, 1864, to keep Sherman's troops from taking Atlanta. The Confederate troops fortified the heights of the mountain, and held off the attacking forces with cannons, rifles and even rocks until the Union troops went around the mountain, and the rebels were forced to pull back.

Kennesaw Mountain National Battlefield Park is one of the few Civil War sites to escape commercial and residential development; Union Veterans from Illinois bought a section of the park to install a monument, and other veterans groups joined in to purchase plots of their own. The site was later presented to the National Park Service.

The park is open daily, from 7:30 am to dusk. There is no admission fee. Take I-75 north to Exit 269, go left for 2.1 miles to Old GA Highway 41; turn left and proceed 1.2 miles to Stilesboro Road. Turn right onto Stilesboro Road, then left into the parking lot. See page 83 for Civil War Museum information.

Peachtree Creek

The Battle of Peachtree Creek took place on what is today an area roughly bounded by I-75, Howell Mill, Northside Drive, Collier Road, Peachtree Creek and Peachtree Road. This area, just south of Buckhead, is known as Brookwood Hills. There are battle markers on Collier Road at Tanyard Creek Park and on the grounds of Piedmont Hospital. Unlike Kennesaw Mountain, this area is a fully developed residential and business district within the city.

Ezra Church

The Battle of Ezra Church occurred on July 28, 1864, when Southern troops engaged Sherman's soldiers on the west side of Atlanta to prevent them from cutting the rail line. The battle on July 28 ranged from I-20 west to Ashby Street, Bankhead Highway to Anderson Avenue, Ezra Church Drive to Chappell Road, west of what is now the Centennial Park area.

Jonesboro

The Battle of Jonesboro was the last of the Battle of Atlanta skirmishes, fought August 31 to September 1, 1864. General Sherman was determined to capture the last remaining rail line out of Atlanta. The stone rail depot on Main Street in Jonesboro was erected in 1868 to replace the one burned by the

Yankees in 1864. The downtown historic district has many markers detailing the surge of fighting through the area.

The Jonesboro battle, as well as the earlier skirmishes around Atlanta, were all costly defeats for the South. After Jonesboro, General Hood's beaten army evacuated the area and left it to be occupied by General Sherman's troops. Atlanta was surrendered by Major James M. Calhoun, September 2, 1864, at what is today the intersection of Northside Drive and Marietta Street.

The African-American Legacy

Atlanta has a rich and distinguished legacy of African-American contributions, both political and economic, not only to Atlanta but to the nation. The most notable among these is Dr. Martin Luther King, Jr., who was born in a Victorian house on Auburn Avenue in 1929, but Auburn Avenue's African-American legacy began long before that.

After the Civil War, former slaves bought property east of the city's central business district, on what was then Wheat Street, a busy east-west thoroughfare. In 1893, citizens petitioned the city council to change the name of Wheat Street to **Auburn Avenue**, which was thought to be more stylish. And stylish it would become. Business executives and factory workers alike took pride in their surroundings, putting up residences, office buildings and places of worship. Auburn Avenue became a mixture of young and old, prominent and obscure, and – until the onset of racial trouble in the early 1900s – black and white.

Auburn Avenue Tour

A walk down Auburn Avenue is an experience rich in African-American history and culture. A national historic district has been created to help maintain the atmosphere of the Sweet Auburn community. Buildings within this district include The Martin Luther King, Jr., Birth Home, the Charles L. Harper Home, The King Center, the Gravesite, Ebenezer Baptist Church, Wheat Street Baptist Church, the Herndon Building, Sweet Auburn Curb Market, the Royal Peacock Club, the Butler Street YMCA, and APEX Museum.

The **Martin Luther King, Jr. Birth Home** at 501 Auburn Avenue. Built in 1895, the Queen Anne-style house has been restored to its appearance during the years 1929, when King was born, to 1941, when his family moved to a house on Boulevard.

Charles L. Harper Home, 535 Auburn Avenue. Constructed in about 1895, this was home to Professor Harper, who lived here from 1910 to 1945, and who was principal of Atlanta's first public high school for the black community, Booker T. Washington High.

The King Center was founded in 1968 by Coretta Scott King and others, to continue the work of Dr. King. The organization works on projects to promote economic and social equality. Today the organization is headed by King's son, Dexter Scott King (see pages 62-63 for more information).

The Martin Luther King, Jr. **Gravesite** was moved in the early 1970s from Southview Cemetery to a site next to the Ebenezer Baptist Church. The present memorial tomb was dedicated in 1977.

Ebenezer Baptist Church, 407-13 Auburn Avenue, was the location from which Martin Luther King, Jr. preached his very first sermon, and served as co-pastor from 1960 to 1968.

The **Wheat Street Baptist Church**, 365 Auburn Avenue, built in 1920, is so called because the original structure was built prior to the name change of the street to Auburn Avenue. The church has been a community institution for decades.

The **Herndon Building**, 231-45 Auburn Avenue (not to be confused with the Herndon Home), a multi-use structure, was named for Alonzo P. Herndon, the ex-slave and founder of the Atlanta Life Insurance Company.

Sweet Auburn Curb Market, 209 Edgewood Avenue, completed in 1923, has been a fresh produce market for both blacks and whites, even during the years of legal segregation.

The **Royal Peacock Club**, 184-86 Auburn Avenue, was known as the Top Hat until 1946, and has featured such well-known entertainers as Cab Calloway, Louis Armstrong, and Aretha Franklin.

Butler Street YMCA, 20-24 Butler Street, was founded in the basement of the Wheat Street Church and has served as an activist location and meeting place.

The **APEX (African American Panoramic Experience) Museum,** 135 Auburn Avenue, includes a replica of an Atlanta streetcar, in which visitors sit to watch a film that tells the story of Auburn Avenue. Exhibits include African and slavery-era artifacts and a recreation of a black-owned drug store on Auburn Avenue (see page 72 for more information).

Spectator Sports

Atlanta is a sports town. Four major league teams (baseball, basketball, football and hockey) call Atlanta home, and the city embraces them all. The most recent entry, the Atlanta Thrashers Hockey Team, drew a crowd of thousands just for the unveiling of the team jersey. This is a city that chants to the "tomahawk chop" at Braves baseball games and dances the "dirty bird" when the Falcons make a touchdown.

College sports also have particularly loyal fans and can be positively rabid for Georgia Tech basketball.

Tickets to most major sporting events can be purchased through Ticketmaster (☎ 404-249-6400 or, outside of Georgia, ☎ 800-326-4000). Locations of Ticketmaster include Tower Records and Publix Supermarkets. You may also purchase from the web at www.ticketmaster.com.

Baseball

ATLANTA BRAVES
Turner Field, 755 Hank Aaron Drive
Atlanta, GA
☎ 404-522-7630

The Atlanta Braves, 1995 World Champions, and 1991 and 1992 National League Champions, play their home games at Turner Field ("the Ted"), built for the 1996 Olympics, from April to October. The Braves are almost as much of a legend as Scarlett O'Hara, having gone from "worst to first" in the National League.

The stadium is a short distance south of Downtown, and is easiest to reach by taking one of several buses from MARTA's Five Points or West End stations; cost for the ride is $1.50 or free with a MARTA transfer. There is also a shuttle bus on game days. Go early and enjoy this old-time-style stadium, with interactive games, an outdoor bar and restaurant, and the Ivan Allen Jr. Braves Museum. This facility has over 4,000 square feet of baseball memorabilia, including the bat "Hammerin Hank" Aaron used to hit his record-breaking 715th home run (see *Museums*, page 73).

Football

ATLANTA FALCONS
Georgia Dome
Atlanta, GA
☎ 404-223-8000

The Atlanta Falcons play in the Georgia Dome, the 71,000-seat stadium that hosted the Superbowl in January, 2000. This massive downtown stadium is as tall as a 27-story building and covers 8.6 acres. Join with the crowd in dancing "the dirty bird" whenever the Falcons score a touchdown.

Basketball

ATLANTA HAWKS
Philips Arena
Atlanta, GA
☎ 404-233-8000

The Atlanta Hawks are the National Basketball Association's team in Atlanta, although not a particularly good one. The team shares the roost at the new

Sunup to Sundown

Philips Arena with the Atlanta Thrashers Hockey team. The regular season runs from October to April.

Hockey

THE ATLANTA THRASHERS
Philips Arena
Atlanta, GA
☎ 404-584-7825

The Atlanta Thrashers debuted in the 1999-2000 NHL season with a dismal record, but the fans didn't care. Collectively this is a city that doesn't know a Zamboni from a blue line, but it doesn't matter; the city has a new sports team to cheer.

Bicycle Racing

DICK LANE VELODROME
1889 Lexington Avenue
East Point, GA
☎ 404-765-1085

South of Atlanta, just a short distance from the Hartsfield Atlanta International Airport, this location draws both amateur and professional bicycle racers. Classes are held on Tuesday and Thursday evenings.

Golf

There are three major golf tournaments played in and around Atlanta each year.

The four-day **PGA BellSouth Classic**, usually held in March at the Tournament Players Club in Duluth, attracts the nation's best golfers. For tickets and information, call ☎ 770-951-8777.

The **Senior PGA Tournament** takes place in September at the Country Club of Georgia near Alpharetta. This event draws up to 40,000 spectators a year. Past players have included Jack Nicklaus, Arnold Palmer, and Chi Chi Rodriguez; call the club at ☎ 770-664-8644 for information.

A word of advice about the **Masters Tournament**: don't expect to get tickets. Tournament tickets are sold to a "patron list," which was closed due to demand in 1972. The "waiting list" to get on the "patron's list" was closed in 1978. The only way to get a ticket to the Masters is to know someone. Tickets to practice sessions are available, but only by mail, not at the gate. The tournament is scheduled so that the play ends on the second Sunday in April. For additional information, call the Augusta National Golf Club at ☎ 706-667-6000.

Horse Racing

THE ATLANTA STEEPLECHASE
Cartersville, GA
☎ 404-237-7436

Held annually on the second weekend in April, this event draws Atlanta's elite. Come to see the Rolls Royces and parade of women's hats at this Ascot-like equestrian event. Cartersville is about 50 minutes north of Atlanta. To reach the racetrack, take I-75 north to Exit 288, onto Route 13 west. Proceed for about three miles. Call for ticket information.

Sunup to Sundown

Polo

ATLANTA POLO CLUB
Majors Road at Post Road
Cumming, GA
☎ 770-316-9109

Every Sunday from June through October, the Atlanta Polo Club holds matches and tournaments. Admission is by the carload ($15), so bring some friends and a picnic. To reach the Polo Club, go north on I-85 to Exit 87, onto Route 400-N (this road becomes Highway 19) to Cumming.

Auto & Motorcycle Racing

THE ATLANTA MOTOR SPEEDWAY
1500 US 41
Hampton, GA
☎ 770-946-4211 or 707-7904, www.gospeedway.com

The site of the NASCAR Coca-Cola 500 and many other events, is just 20 miles south of Atlanta. When Richard Petty retired in 1992, a crowd of more than 168,000 fans came out to witness his final race. Just make sure you remember where you parked your car; finding it later in the dark could be a daunting experience.

A major rebuild of the facility was completed in 2000. Atlanta Motor Speedway is home to two NASCAR Winston Cup races; one is in mid-March, and the second, the final cup race of the year, is held in mid-November.

The Speedway is about 30 miles south of downtown Atlanta. To get there, take I-75 south to Exit 235;

keep right onto Tara Boulevard (Hwy 41-S) and proceed about 15 miles to Hampton.

ROAD ATLANTA
5300 Winder Highway
Braselton, GA
☎ 770-967-6143 (information) or 800-849-7223 (tickets), www.roadatlanta.com

Road Atlanta was rebuilt and modernized in 1999. It is home to an American Le Mans Series race, the Petit Le Mans, held in late September. It also hosts an all-womens' GT Racing Series. In addition, the American Motorcycle Association and the Sports Car Club of America hold regular races here. To get to the facility, which is about 50 miles northeast of downtown Atlanta, take I-85 north to Exit 129, onto Route 53; proceed west on 53 for five miles.

Recreation

Atlanta's moderate climate allows nearly year-round participation in sports and outdoor activities. You'll find Atlantans participating in everything from baseball to street hockey. Don't forget that the climate during the summer months can be excessively hot and humid. Whatever your game, be sure to drink plenty of fluids.

Bicycling

The city has very few designated bicycle paths. The safest place to cycle is within **Piedmont Park**, which is closed to vehicle traffic. Bikes can be rented from Skate Escape, across from the park at 1086 Piedmont.

Canoeing & Rafting

The **Chattahoochee Outdoor Center**, 1990 Island Ford Parkway, ☎ 770-395-3861, www.chattahoocheerafting.com, rents canoes by the day, and runs a convenient shuttle bus between the put-in and take-out points. Canoes rent for approximately $35 a day, with a $100 deposit required. The center is open daily from Memorial Day through Labor Day. See page 86 for directions to the Island Ford Unit of the National Recreation Area.

Golf

The only public course within sight of Downtown is the **Bobby Jones Golf Course**, 384 Woodward Way, ☎ 404-355-1009, which is named for the famed Atlanta golfer. This exceedingly popular 18-hole, par 71 course, is on a portion of the Battle of Peachtree Creek site (see page 92).

Most of the golf courses are located outside of the Perimeter; see the *Beyond Atlanta* section, pages 210-213, for more courses.

Tennis

Tennis is huge in Metro Atlanta. The city maintains 50 tennis court locations; one of the largest and easiest to find is the **Piedmont Park Tennis Center**. With 12 courts, a pro shop, and racquet stringing facilities, this is one of the most comprehensive locations. The center is open Mondays through Fridays, 11 am to 9 pm; Saturdays, 9 am to 6 pm; Sundays, 9:30 am to 7 pm. The fee is $1.50 per person, per hour, before 6pm, and $1.75 per hour afterwards.

Shop Till You Drop

From Downtown to Buckhead and beyond, you'll discover an amazing array of locations to shop and spend. Haute couture, antiques, mega-malls and specialty shops in Atlanta's neighborhoods all conspire to separate your money from your wallet.

Atlanta is the Hong Kong of shopping in the Southeast. According to the Atlanta Convention & Visitors Bureau, Atlanta has more shopping center space than any city but Chicago. At last count, Metro Atlanta had 53 malls. Atlanta also has many specific shopping "districts" for those hot on the trail of antiques, art and decorative objects.

Most stores and malls are open Monday to Saturday from 10 am-9 pm, and Sundays from noon until 6 pm, except where noted. Most Downtown stores are closed on Sunday, except for those around the tourist draws such as Underground Atlanta and the CNN Center.

Malls

Downtown & Vicinity

Shopping in the downtown area is largely limited to tourist trinkets and services for office workers. Notable exceptions are listed below.

UNDERGROUND ATLANTA
Upper Alabama and Peachtree Streets

Underground Atlanta features over 40 stores, including national chains such as **Eddie Bauer**, **The Gap**, and **Sam Goody**. Local specialty shops such as **Hats Under Atlanta**, **Habersham Winery**, and the very unusual **Art By God**, which includes an array of items from fossils to artistic creations by Native Americans. Underground is far more than shopping; you'll discover restaurants and nightlife as well. When you need some respite, stop at the **Café Du Monde** for New Orleans-style beignets and authentic French coffee laced with chicory.

MACY'S
180 Peachtree Street
Atlanta, GA
☎ 404-221-7221

This is the one and only department store remaining in the downtown core. Marble floors and chandeliers evoke the grandeur of days gone by, but you'll find the contents up to the millisecond. If you are at a convention or doing business, and you've neglected to pack something significant (wing tips, perhaps?), your best bet to find the item is at Macy's. The selection of business clothing is quite good, and the ground floor accessories selection is particularly outstanding.

THE MALL AT PEACHTREE CENTER
231 Peachtree St.
Atlanta, GA
☎ 404-524-3787

Peachtree Center sprawls above and below ground with over 30 shops, restaurants and services right in the heart of the city. Brooks Brothers, stationers, shoes, etc; if you forgot to pack it for your trip, it's a good bet you'll find it here. The mall is closed on Sundays.

CNN CENTER
Marietta Street at Techwood Drive
Atlanta, GA
☎ 404-827-4791

If you can't leave home without Braves, Hawks, Falcons or Thrasher team regalia, or a memento of *Gone With The Wind*, you'll be sure to find it at the Atlanta Shop, Braves Clubhouse, or The Turner Store. There's a very good food court, and an outstanding British pub, Reggie's, on site (see *Best Places to Eat*, page 133).

Midtown

ANSLEY MALL
Piedmont and Monroe

A lively little neighborhood mall, north of Piedmont Park, with grocery, drug and service stores. A real treat is the wine store, with a comprehensive selection. You'll find a Radio Shack, hardware store, card store, health foods and lots of places to find those "I forgot to pack" items. Ansley Mall is open Mondays-Saturdays, 10-8, and Sundays, 10-5.

RIO MALL
595 Piedmont Avenue at North Avenue

Just four blocks north of the Civic Center near the Fox Theatre, Rio Mall offers an assortment of clothiers, galleries, restaurants, services and nightspots. The mall is about to undergo some major renovations. Rio Mall is open Mondays-Saturdays, 10-8, and Sundays, 12-6.

COLONY SQUARE MALL
Colony Square, 14th & Peachtree

Food courts, business services and restaurants in the Piedmont Park area. Currently quite limited, but the mall is renovating and adding new dimensions. Country Place restaurant is a delightful start to an evening at the symphony or theater, with its upscale and innovative American cuisine. The Woodruff Arts Center is just across the street, so you will have to park only once for both dinner and your night out. Colony Square is open Mondays-Fridays, 10-6; Saturdays and Sundays, 12-6.

⊚ TIP

The best mall alternative is downtown Decatur. The business district clustered around the old courthouse, at Commerce Drive and Church Street, is filled with a variety of stores offering everything from housewares to gardening supplies to books and clothes. Take MARTA to the Decatur station.

Buckhead

Buckhead is the South's Beverly Hills wannabee. The area is home to some of the city's most prestigious neighborhoods, and the shopping centers and stores are an upscale reflection. If you are a serious shopper, this is the place to begin. Don't let the proliferation of stores such as Tiffany, Gucci, and other wallet-swallowing stores deter you, there are bargains to be had. Let's begin with the malls.

PHIPPS PLAZA
3500 Peachtree Road, NE
☎ 404-262-0992 or 800-810-7700
Hours: Mondays-Saturdays, 10-9, Sundays 12-5:30
MARTA: Buckhead or Lenox

Housed inside a center designed to resemble a Georgian mansion, you'll find Atlanta's only Saks Fifth Avenue, Lord and Taylor, Tiffany and Parisian heading the list of over 100 stores. Phipps is upper crust. They even offer valet parking and a concierge. The Verandah Food Court and a multiplex cinema round out the Phipps Experience.

LENOX SQUARE
3393 Peachtree Road at Lenox Road
☎ 404-233-6767
Hours: Mondays-Saturdays, 10-9, Sundays 12-6
MARTA: Buckhead or Lenox

The grande dame of Atlanta's malls, the largest in the Southeast, is anchored by Rich's, Macy's, and Neiman Marcus. New additions include Crate & Barrel and Restoration Hardware. The mall had a recent face-lift, and you'll find it a light and airy place to shop and schmooze. More than 250 shops and eateries (including Brasserie Le Côze, listed on page 181) will keep you busy for hours.

Sunup to Sundown

Phipps Plaza and Lenox Square operate a shuttle service to ferry shoppers from one mall to another. You'll need to park only once for this mega-shopping experience.

⊘ TIP

Don't even think of driving or parking at Phipps Plaza or Lenox Square during the height of the Christmas shopping season, unless you plan to pack a lunch for the traffic jams. Instead, take MARTA to the Lenox Square stop.

Antiques & Rarities

Buckhead

Bennett Street

Home to a large assortment of antique and decorative arts dealers, there's no junk to be found here. These shops are definitely of the better quality. Three blocks north of Piedmont Hospital, on the west side of Peachtree Road, it is easily reached by taking the #23 bus from Arts Center, Lenox or Buckhead stations. The shops listed are open Mondays-Saturdays, 10 am-5 pm.

BITTERSWEET LTD.
45 Bennett St. NW
☎ 404-351-6594

Bittersweet offers a fine selection of English and sporting antiques such as handcrafted wooden pond yachts and fishing poles.

THE STALLS
116 Bennett St. NW
☎ 404-352-4430

Here you'll find 70-plus dealers, with stalls designed as though they are waiting for the photographer from House Beautiful. You'll find everything from tapestries to crystal inkwells; doorknobs to oil paintings.

SHOPS AT BEAMAN'S
BEAMAN'S ANTIQUES
25 Bennett St., NW
☎ 404-352-9388

A select group of merchants with an eclectic inventory is housed under one roof. English antique furnishings, Chinese deco rugs, religious icons and antique timepieces are just a few of the treasures awaiting discovery.

OUT OF THE WOODS
22-B Bennett St., NW
☎ 404-351-0446

The shop features wood, wood and more wood. In addition, Tibetan singing bowls, Haitian oil drum art and Ukrainian eggshell jewelry are offered.

Paces Ferry
One of my favorite clusters of Buckhead shops can be found in the area of Roswell and West Paces Ferry Roads. To reach the area by car, take Peachtree Street north towards Buckhead. At the Paces Ferry Road intersection, go straight through onto Roswell Road (Peachtree Street bears to the right). Find a spot to park and enjoy this little confluence of strees with boutique shops.

BOXWOOD GARDENS AND GIFTS
100 East Andrews Drive NE
☎ 404-233-3400
Hours: Mondays-Saturdays, 10-6

This is a very popular stop for floral arrangements, art and antiques, between West Paces Ferry and Roswell.

C'EST MOI
3198 Paces Ferry Place NW
☎ 404-467-0095
Hours: Mondays-Saturdays, 10-5:30

Stop here for pottery, linens, furnishings and unusual children's gifts, just off East Andrews.

THE PLANTATION SHOP
3193 Roswell Road
☎ 404-239-1866
Hours: Mondays-Saturdays, 10-6

This is the place to go for special presents, such as weddings gifts. Oodles of antiques and reproductions are offered at reasonable prices. You'll also find Majolica and lamps.

THE SIGNATURE SHOP AND GALLERY
3267 Roswell Road
☎ 404-237-4426
Hours: Tuesdays-Saturdays, 10-5:30

Lots of one-of-a-kind objects are featured, such as wood bowls, pottery and textile arts.

Miami Circle

There are over 80 stores in Miami Circle, a decorator-favorite street in the Buckhead area. The neighborhood is easily reached from MARTA's Lindbergh

Station. If you drive, take Piedmont Road north toward Buckhead; when you pass Sidney Marcus Boulevard, Miami Circle is the first right after the Cub Foods shopping center. Some of the highlights include the following shops.

BOOKS & CASES & PRINTS ETC.
800 Miami Circle NE
Atlanta, GA
☎ 404-231-9107
Hours: Mondays-Saturdays, 10-5:30

The shop specializes in decorative bindings, prints and rare books, and perfect accents for any room.

> ### ⊚ *TIP*
>
> Hungry? Try **Eclipse Di Luna**, 764 Miami Circle, ☎ 404-846-0449, for sandwiches, soups, and traditional Spanish tapas.

JEWELL TOUCH
764 Miami Circle NE
Atlanta, GA
☎ 404-869-6077
Hours: Mondays-Saturdays, 10-4:30

Custom bedding and linens from around the world are sold here.

MAISON DE PROVENCE
764 Miami Circle NE
Atlanta, GA
☎ 404-364-0205
Hours: Mondays-Saturdays, 10-5

The owners live in Provence, France and are able to shop all year long for the antique Country French furniture that fills the shop. It's enough to make you want to buy a villa and retire out of the country.

MAURICE CHANDELIER
715 Miami Circle NE
Atlanta, GA
☎ 404-237-5402
Hours: Mondays-Saturdays, 10-5

This shop will certainly light up your day with more than 500 antique lighting fixtures on display.

Other Antiques Markets

Cheshire Bridge Road

Nestled amongst the lingerie "modeling" businesses and the restaurants are many antique dealers. The larger shops rent out space to smaller dealers, so you'll never be quite sure what rests inside any particular shop. Cheshire Bridge Road is between Piedmont and La Vista Roads.

Outside Atlanta

CHAMBLEE'S ANTIQUES ROW
Broad Street and Peachtree Road
Chamblee, GA
☎ 770-458-1614
Hours: Mondays-Saturdays, 10-5
MARTA: Chamblee Station, or I-85 north to Chamblee Tucker Road

More than 200 antique dealers have gathered in this architecturally interesting shopping district northeast of Buckhead. Old homes, churches and stores all sell antiques and collectibles. Antiques Row is within walking distance of the Chamblee Station MARTA stop; you can also reach the Row by the #25

Tilly Mill bus. The area looks a little shabby, but you'll find treasures inside.

LAKEWOOD ANTIQUES MARKET
Lakewood Fairgrounds
2000 Lakewood Avenue SW
☎ 404-622-4488
Hours: Fridays and Saturdays, 9-6; Sundays 10-5

An exceptionally popular market, held on the second weekend of each month, it features thousands of unusual antiques and collectibles. Admission is $3; children 12 and under are admitted free. The market is open Friday, Saturday and Sunday, but there's a special early buyers day on Thursday, when the admission is $5. Take I-75/85 south from Downtown; exit at the Lakewood Freeway East, and follow the signs.

Vintage & Consignment

Used clothing is not generally at the top of a traveler's shopping list but Atlanta is worthy of being an exception. This is a very dressy, clothes-conscious city, so the finds are quite good.

CONSIGNSHOP
Toco Hills Shopping Center
2899-A N. Druid Hills Road NE
Atlanta
☎ 404-633-6257
Hours: Mondays-Saturdays, 10-6; Sundays, 12-6

Consignshop caters to both genders with quality clothing. There's even a maternity selection.

ELEGANCE RESALE
3330 Piedmont Road NE
Buckhead
☎ 404-233-8996
Hours: Mondays-Saturdays, 12:30-4

Elegance Resale has been in business for more than 15 years, offering costume jewelry and women's designer fashions. Located in the Piedmont Peachtree Crossing shopping center.

JUNKMAN'S DAUGHTER
464 Moreland Avenue
☎ 404-577-3188
Hours: Mondays-Fridays, 11-7; Saturdays, 11-8; Sundays, 12-7

You can't miss this location in the heart of Little Five Points, with it's space-age mural front in brilliant blue. Shop here for vintage and new clothing, housewares and all kinds of accessories. It's sort of like a Target store for aging hippies and hippie wannabees.

PSYCHO SISTERS
5952 Roswell Road NE
Sandy Springs
☎ 404-255-5578
Hours: Mondays-Fridays, 11-7; Sundays, 11-5

The place to buy "cool" clothes at cheap prices. It's radical chic where you would least expect to find it. You can buy, sell or trade.

Books & Bookstores

Downtown & Vicinity

BARNES & NOBLE
2900 Peachtree Road NW
Buckhead
☎ 404-261-7747
Hours: Sundays-Thursdays, 9 am-11 pm; Fridays
and Saturdays, 9 am-midnight

You can get books, magazines, CDs and hot coffee in
the Starbucks that's attached. This Peachtree location is wood paneled and has a traditional library
feel.

GEORGIA BOOK STORE
124 Edgewood Avenue NE
☎ 404-659-0959
Hours: Mondays-Thursdays, 9-6; Fridays, 9-5

Although it's primarily a textbook store for Georgia
State University, located adjacent to the campus,
you will also find sports-related items and local and
regional souvenirs.

Georgia Book Store still has memorabilia from the 1996 Olympic Games.

SHRINE OF THE BLACK MADONNA
946 Ralph Abernathy Boulevard
☎ 404-752-6125
Hours: Mondays, 3-7 pm; Tuesdays-Saturdays, 11-
7; Sundays, 1:45-3 pm

In the West End, you'll find this to be an excellent location for books on the African-American experience
for both children and adults.

TWO FRIENDS BOOKSTORE
598 Cascade Road
☎ 404-758-7711
Hours: Mondays-Saturdays, 11-6

This African-American bookstore sells figurines and original signed and numbered prints, as well as books. Coffee is free to customers, and the store holds book signings once or twice a month.

Midtown

OUTWRITE
991 Piedmont Road NE
☎ 404-607-0082
Hours: Sundays-Thursdays, 8 am-11 pm; Fridays-Saturdays, 8 am-midnight

Selling gay and lesbian books, cards, and magazines, this shop on the corner of Tenth Street and Piedmont Road also has a coffee shop.

Buckhead

BORDERS BOOKS AND MUSIC
3637 Peachtree Road NE
☎ 404-237-0707
Hours: Mondays-Saturdays, 9 am-11 pm; Sundays, 9 am-10 pm

Directly across the road from Phipps Plaza, this location features an espresso bar/café and book signings with both local and celebrity authors. Oh yes, there are lots of books, too, spread out over approximately 35,000 square feet. A good place to find out-of-town newspapers and foreign language periodicals.

CHAPTER 11, THE DISCOUNT BOOKSTORE
Peachtree Battle Shopping Center
2345 Peachtree Road
☎ 404-237-7199
Hours: Mondays-Thursdays, 10-10; Fridays & Saturdays, 10-11; Sundays, 11-7

All of the books are discounted by, you guessed it, at least 11%. The selections are good and the book signings are plentiful.

Little Five Points

CHARIS BOOKS
1189 Euclid Avenue
☎ 404-524-0304
Hours: Daily, 10:30-6

Feminist books, gay and lesbian literature, and children's books are the focus of this shop. The store sponsors weekly community-oriented programs that frequently highlight readings by noted authors.

Druid Hills & Decatur

TALL TALES
Toco Hills Shopping Center
2999 N. Druid Hills Rd. NE
☎ 404-636-2498
Hours: Mondays-Saturdays, 9:30-9:30; Sundays, 12:30-6:30

A full service, independent bookstore in the Emory University area, specializing in children's books and works of fiction. What makes Tall Tales truly special is the level of service it provides. The staff graciously searches out hard-to-find items, and gets orders filled with a promptness that borders on magical.

Final Touch Gallery & Books is especially noted for its lavish book signings, which have catered food and fresh flowers.

FINAL TOUCH GALLERY & BOOKS
133 East Court Street
Decatur, GA
☎ 404-378-5300
Hours: Mondays-Saturdays, 10-6

An independent bookseller (one of the last standing) that stocks music, toys, gifts and collectibles in a spacious two-story house on the Courthouse Square. The cookbook section is particularly extensive.

Sybaritic Atlanta

Day Spas

Travel can take its toll on you with stress and tension. If you need a time out and a little pampering (or a lot), Atlanta can meet your most demanding spa requirements.

Expect to pay from $55 to $100 for a facial; full-day packages can cost anywhere from $175 to $270, but most fall into the range of $110 to $150, depending upon the services offered.

SPA SYDELL
Buckhead Plaza, 3060 Peachtree Road NW
☎ 404-237-2505
Hours: Mondays-Saturdays, 9-9; Sundays, 11-7

Spa Sydell is the best known of the spas in Atlanta. Specialties include a massage for two, makeup consultations, and hairdos. A day at the spa includes lunch from some of the best restaurants in the city. If you need to feel like a visiting glitterati, this is the place to come.

JOLIE, THE DAY SPA
3619 Piedmont Road, NE
☎ 404-266-0060
Hours: Mondays-Saturdays, 9-6; Sundays, 11-5

Full- and half-day spa packages are available; services include a variety of treatments from aromatherapy mud wraps, seaweed cellulite treatments, and four-layer facials.

QUINTESSENCE, A DAY SPA
3220 Peachtree Street
☎ 404-364-0474
Hours: Mondays-Wednesdays, 10-6; Thursdays and Fridays, 10-7; Saturdays 10-6

Housed in what was once the Mexican Embassy, this spa is an oasis in the hubbub that is Buckhead. Facial treatments, hand and foot therapy, massage therapy, and waxing are among the services offered. The treatment rooms are softly lit, and the custom pedicure chairs are pure heaven.

Sunup to Sundown

Overnight

THE SPA AT CHATEAU ELAN
Haven Harbor Drive
Braselton, GA
☎ 770-271-6064, www.chateauelan.com/spa

This spa is outside the Perimeter, but you'll find it worth the trip. Modeled after a European health spa, it's a part of the Château Elan complex (see page 201), about an hour's drive northeast of Atlanta. This is the only spa in the area where you can stay overnight, or for several days. In addition to a full range of spa treatments, you can get an individual fitness assessment as well as a personalized exercise prescription. This makes a wonderful weekend retreat after a full conference schedule.

Suggested Itineraries

For One Day

It's more than possible to see the highlights of Atlanta in just one day, if you don't mind spending a limited amount of time at each of the attractions or historic sites.

Begin with **Underground Atlanta** and the **World of Coca-Cola** for a taste of both the old and the new. Then walk east on Martin Luther King, Jr. Drive to the **Georgia State Capitol** for a guided tour of the gold-domed building. Walk north on **Piedmont Avenue**, catch a west-bound MARTA train at the Georgia State station and ride two stops to the **OMNI-Dome-GWCC** (Georgia World Congress Center) station. It's just a short walk along Techwood Drive to the **CNN Center.** The food court area inside the CNN Center is a good place to take a break for a fast lunch. If you want to linger and watch for familiar broadcasting faces, try **Reggie's British Pub** (see page 133).

From the CNN Center, cross Marietta Street and walk along International Boulevard through **Centennial Olympic Park**, with its commemorative brick walkways and fountains. Have your camera ready for some wonderful Atlanta skyline photos.

Continue along to Peachtree Street and take a break for some shopping at **Macy's** or **Peachtree Center**. To get a taste of the exhibits that await within the

High Museum of Art, you can walk south on Peachtree Street and stop at the **Georgia-Pacific Building** to view the exhibits in the Museum's **Folk Arts** and **Photography Galleries**.

Stroll south past the Candler and Flatiron buildings to **Robert W. Woodruff Memorial Park**.

Before returning to your hotel you could try **Dailey's Restaurant**, at 17 International Boulevard. This is a shadowy, somewhat noisy and altogether pleasant eatery featuring creative American fare.

For a Weekend

On the first day, start with **Underground Atlanta**, the **World of CocaCola** and the **CNN Center**. Then, after lunch proceed to the **Martin Luther King, Jr. Historic District** and the adjacent neighborhood of **Sweet Auburn**. It's just three stops on MARTA from the OMNI/Dome/GWCC station to the MLK Memorial station.

Begin at the **Martin Luther King, Jr. National Historic District Visitors Center** to view the powerful exhibits reflecting the Civil Rights Movement and the life of Dr. King.

Follow along to the **Martin Luther King, Jr. Birth Home**, the **Martin Luther King, Jr. Center for Nonviolent Social Change**, where you may view the tomb of Dr. King, and the nearby **Ebenezer Baptist Church**, also on Auburn Avenue, where he preached his very first sermon.

Take time to stroll through the **Sweet Auburn** district to absorb the flavor of this historic, predominantly African-American neighborhood.

Sunup to Sundown

While in the Cyclorama, look for the figure of Clark Gable that was added in the 1940s, due to repeated requests by visitors.

The next day, begin with a trip to the **Atlanta Cyclorama** in historic **Grant Park**. Follow that with a visit to **Zoo Atlanta** to view the recently acquired giant pandas.

For Five Days

Start with the weekend itinerary as your base, and begin the third day with a trip to Buckhead to see the **Atlanta History Center**, with its comprehensive exhibits, restored houses and landscaped grounds.

To get there, take MARTA to the Buckhead station; don't forget to ask for a bus transfer. Outside the station take the #23 bus heading south to West Paces Ferry Road (you may also get the #23 bus northbound from the Arts Center station). Walk west of Paces Ferry Road for about ½ mile to Andrews Drive.

If you are driving from downtown Atlanta, take Peachtree Street north to the intersection of Paces Ferry Road (be sure to stay in the left lane as you approach the intersection; Peachtree Street will bear right). Take a left onto Paces Ferry Road and proceed about ½ mile to Andrews Drive.

A good stop for lunch in Buckhead is the Swan Coach House, 3130 Slaton Drive NW, on the grounds of the Atlanta History Center.

After lunch take time to stroll through Buckhead and its array of shops, or drive along West Paces Ferry Road to view Buckhead's array of opulent mansions.

Complete the tour with a foray to Buckhead's companion shopping centers, **Phipps Plaza** and **Lenox Square**. Finish off the day with dinner in Buckhead at one of the many trendy restaurants and nightspots (see *Best Places to Eat*, pages 176-188).

Days four and five can be spent on attractions just outside of the city. You can easily spend a full day at **Kennesaw Mountain National Battlefield Park** (see page 91), northwest of Atlanta on I-75 towards Marietta, where Rebel and Union soldiers battled in June, 1864.

During the summer months, a night out at **Chastain Park** (just north of Buckhead on Powers Ferry Road), hearing a concert at the open-air amphitheater, is an excellent way to spend an evening.

Château Elan, a winery, resort, and golf course about an hour northeast of Atlanta in Braselton, offers winery tours; call for information (see page 201).

You might also want to include an excursion to **Stone Mountain Park,** a 3,200-acre family recreational facility built around the largest exposed mass of granite on earth. At this park, located 16 miles east of downtown Atlanta, you'll find the world's largest sculpture, the Confederate Memorial, a bas-relief carving of Confederate President Jefferson Davis and generals Robert E. Lee and Stonewall Jackson (see *Attractions*, page 203 for details).

Just east of the downtown area, **The Carter Presidential Center**, on Freedom Parkway in the Little Five Points area, and the **Fernbank Museum of Natural History** and its IMAX Theater, in Druid Hills, are also worthy of morning or afternoon visits.

After Dark

Atlanta may be the new hip-hop capital, but that doesn't mean that you won't find music and a place that suits your individual style. Atlanta shines at night with an astonishing array of nightlife. From jazz to country, string quartets to salsa bands, Atlanta has it all.

Performing Arts

Atlanta has worked hard to achieve its current position as the cultural capital of the South and has diligently applied itself to all aspects of the arts. From symphony to jazz to hip-hop you'll find a venue and program to your taste. The city hasn't earned the nickname "Hotlanta" for the climate.

For the most complete listings of current and future cultural events and entertainment, check the *Atlanta Journal-Constitution's* Friday "Weekend Preview" or Saturday "Leisure" sections. *Creative Loafing*, a weekly publication, has the best listings for local music and club scenes.

Dance

ATLANTA BALLET
1400 West Peachtree Street
☎ 404-817-8700

For more than 70 years Atlanta Ballet has been a fixture in the arts community of the city. The company is the oldest continually operating dance company in America, and is the official state ballet company of Georgia. Under the direction of John McFall, recent productions have included *Dracula*, *Coppelia*, *Swan Lake* and, seasonally, of course, *The Nutcracker*. The company performs its productions at the Fox Theatre.

DANCERS COLLECTIVE
4279 Roswell Road, NE
☎ 404-233-7600

The Dancers Collective provides Atlanta with the only subscription season for contemporary dance. Works have included performances by Bebe Miller, David Dorfman and Susan Marshall and such established groups as Pilobolus and DanceBrazil. The Collective presents its works at diverse venues such as Agnes Scott College and The Rialto Center for the Performing Arts.

Music

ATLANTA OPERA
728 West Peachtree Street NW
☎ 404-881-8801
www.atlantaopera.org

Under the artistic and administrative direction of William Fred Scott and Alfred Kennedy, the Atlanta Opera is now one of the fastest-growing opera companies in the nation. Each year four fully staged operas are produced annually at the Fox Theatre. Recent productions have included *La Boheme*, *Der Rosenkavalier* and *Samson and Delilah*.

ATLANTA SYMPHONY
Woodruff Memorial Arts Center
1280 Peachtree Street
☎ 404-733-5000

In just a little over 50 years, the Atlanta Symphony
has evolved from an inspired group of high school
musicians into a major orchestra with an international reputation and 14 Grammy Awards. The regular season runs from September to May. During
their summer season in July and August, the symphony plays outdoors at the Chastain Amphitheater.

SAVOYARDS MUSICAL THEATRE
3101 Roswell Road
Marietta, GA 30062
☎ 770-565-9651

Known for its performances of Gilbert and Sullivan,
this company, with a 26-piece orchestra, has ex-
panded its repertoire to include other kinds of musical productions. Performances are primarily held at
the Robert Ferst Center for the Arts at Georgia
Tech.

ROBERT FERST CENTER FOR THE ARTS
AT GEORGIA TECH
349 Ferst Drive NW
Atlanta, GA 30332-0468
☎ 404-894-ARTS (2787)

To get to the Georgia Tech campus, take Peachtree
Street to North Avenue; turn west and drive about ½

mile to Tech Parkway; turn right, then right again onto Ferst Drive.

Theater

ACTOR'S EXPRESS
King Plow Arts Center
887 W. Marietta St. NW
☎ 404-875-1606

The company began in a church basement in 1988 and has evolved into one of downtown Atlanta's most respected theater companies. A season usually includes classics, comedies and contemporary dramas.

AGATHA'S – A TASTE OF MYSTERY
693 Peachtree Street NE
☎ 404-875-1610
MARTA: North Avenue Station or Bus #10

Be part of the production at Agatha's! You may be asked to sing a song, speak some lines, or participate with your entire table in some silliness. Don't be shy; it's all part of the experience.

If you can't decide whether to go to dinner or to solve a murder, this is the place. Agatha's has raised "dinner theater" to a new level. You actually are wined and dined with very good food and attentive hosts before the play begins and during the performance. The plays are all "original," although loosely based on recognizable plots. Some recent productions have included *Cat on a Hot Tin Streetcar* and *An Affair To Dismember*.

ALLIANCE THEATER COMPANY
Woodruff Arts Center
1280 Peachtree Street NE
☎ 404-733-5000
MARTA: Arts Center Station

The Southeast's leading professional theater offers performances, backstage tours. Elton John debuted his fraught-with-perils musical, *Elaborate Lives* (based on *Aida*, and co-authored with Tim Rice), at the Alliance. Other more auspicious debuts have included Alfred Uhry's *Last Night of Ballyhoo*, which won a Tony Award in 1996. In the weeks prior to the debut of a new work, the Alliance hosts free "bag lunch" sessions with actors and authors, discussing the work to be performed, usually held at lunchtime. Call for details.

> ⊙ **TIP**
>
> Get a tasty lunch from the café at the High Museum of Art and participate in one of the "bag lunch" sessions with actors and directors at the Alliance Theater. Call the theater for dates and times.

THE FOX THEATRE
660 Peachtree Street NE
☎ 404-817-8700
MARTA: North Avenue Station

Listed on the National Register of Historic Places, this 1929 Moorish/Art Deco fantasy hosts a wide range of live performances plus a summer movie series. Most of the Broadway touring companies bring their shows to the "Fabulous Fox."

After Dark

The Fox did not debut Gone With The Wind in 1939. That honor went to the Loews Theatre, which no longer exists. All that remains is a plaque commemorating that special night on the wall of the Georgia-Pacific building.

Originally planned as the headquarters for the Yaarab Temple of the Ancient Arabic Order of the Nobles of the Mystic Shrine (the Shriners), the project fell on hard times in 1929. In order to complete the structure, a deal was struck with movie magnate William Fox to include a spectacular movie theater and ground level retail space. The Fox opened on Christmas Day in 1929, but after only a little over two years was forced to close. It cost more than $2.75 million dollars to build and was sold at auction for $75,000.

Eventually the theater reopened, and, in the 1940s it became a venue for the Metropolitan Opera when that company toured Atlanta. For years this was a high point of the Atlanta social season. The Met last performed at the Fox in 1968.

By the mid 70s the Fox was once again in danger of being closed and razed to the ground to make way for a new skyscraper. Thousands of Atlantans joined in the work of Atlanta Landmarks to save the Fox, and $1.8 million was raised in time to meet the demolition deadline. The Fox reopened in time to celebrate its 50th anniversary.

⊚ TIP

The limited pitch to the seating on the ground floor of the Fox Theatre can make viewing difficult for those short of stature. Try for a front row loge seat for best viewing.

ATLANTA CIVIC CENTER
395 Piedmont Avenue
☎ 404-523-6275

This Downtown auditorium seats around 5,000 people, and has very clear sight lines. Amplified audio could definitely use some improvement. This is the venue for productions such as *Miss Saigon* and *Showboat*.

Be very careful late at night using the Civic Center MARTA Station or, better yet, take a taxi.

THE NEW ATLANTA SHAKESPEARE TAVERN
499 Peachtree Street NE
☎ 404-874-5299
MARTA: Bus #10 or 99 to Midtown

Enjoy a theatrical romp of an evening here. Swashbuckling and wenchful, you'll feel transported to Shakespeare's own time. The setting is casual, and you'll have to fetch your own food from a small buffet that features British pub-style food such as shepherd's pie and fish and chips. While waiting for the curtain to go up, you'll be entertained by some practice "sword play" or whatever is appropriate. Expect a line; they still haven't quite figured out how to seat patrons quickly and efficiently, but the $15-25 cost is worth the wait.

Bars, Jazz & Dance Clubs

Atlanta has always had a raucous reputation since its early days as railroad town. Today, with its largely under-40 population, the vibrant nightlife continues. Atlanta after dark includes everything from quiet coffeehouses to high-energy techno-dance clubs, acous-

After Dark

tic to grunge, disco to swing or cheek-to-cheek. You'll find clubs all over the city, but party central was, and is, Buckhead.

Downtown Atlanta

BACKSTREET
845 Peachtree Street NE
☎ 404-873-1986

Disco, disco, disco – almost 24 hours a day. Once mostly gay, now pretty mixed.

CHURCHILL GROUNDS
660 Peachtree Street
☎ 404-876-3030

A swank little club cuddled up next door to the Fox Theatre, this has become the place to hear traditional jazz from solid local ensembles. "The vibe is elegant," according to local jazz radio host, Deb Moore, on WCLK.

FANDANGLES
165 Courtland Street NE, in the Sheraton Atlanta Hotel
☎ 404-659-6500

The ultra-modern lounge with Euro-pop music has a bold color scheme and private sitting rooms.

HARD ROCK CAFE
215 Peachtree Street NE
☎ 404-688-7625

Just like all the others – crowded, busy, and over priced. Join the tourists, if you must.

JOCKS 'N JILLS
One CNN Center NW
☎ 404-688-4225

Part of a chain, it's your basic sports bar, with a big burger menu and lots and lots of television sets.

KARMA
79-A Poplar Street
☎ 404-577-6967

Karma is where the beautiful people go in downtown Atlanta. Very, very New York. As you enter beneath the blood-red canopy, you will be reminded of *1001 Nights.*

MUMBO JUMBO
89 Park Place NE
☎ 404-523-0330

Everyone, from bankers to hip-hoppers, converges here. It has a sexy, clubby atmosphere. Absolutely the hippest bar in downtown Atlanta.

REGGIE'S BRITISH PUB
100 Techwood Drive NW
☎ 404-525-1437

A little bit of jolly old England, moved into the CNN Center. Lots of fun on Independence Day when they throw the "losers" a party.

RITZ-CARLTON ATLANTA
181 Peachtree Streets NE
☎ 404-659-0400

Good jazz, great martinis, and a location that will impress anyone.

After Dark

THE TAP ROOM
231 Peachtree Street NE
☎ 404-577-7860

If you have been searching for a high-tech martini, look no further. All a Tap Room bartender must do to pour a near-perfect drink is to pull a lever, and voila! Once the lever is pulled, a spring-activated touch of air shoots the fluid through a frozen tube to a glass waiting only inches away. You won't believe this until you've seen it.

Midtown

BLIND WILLIE'S
828 North Highland Avenue NE
☎ 404-873-2583

It's blues in the night in this smoky house of blues. That next best thing to a Mississippi juke joint.

THE CRESCENT ROOM
1136 Crescent Avenue NE at 13th Street
☎ 404-875-5252

A sophisticated atmosphere marks this upscale place to meet for drinks with Atlanta's smart set.

DARK HORSE TAVERN
816 North Highland Avenue NE
☎ 404-873-3607

For the young, casual crowd, this trés trendy watering hole has live music downstairs, bar food and socializing upstairs. The "Old English" dining room is handy for dinner after libations.

DEUX PLEX
1789 Cheshire Bridge Road NE
☎ 404-733-5900

Anything goes at this madcap and eclectic dance emporium, located north of Piedmont Park. There are Latin nights, fashion shows, art showings, AIDS benefits, chefs' samplings and even a wine tasting or two.

FAT MATT'S RIB SHACK
1811 Piedmont Road NE
☎ 404-607-1622

Live blues bands raise the rafters of this roadhouse. You'll come for the music, but you'll stay for the excellent barbecue. This tiny place can be very busy and very loud. No table service. You order your food in advance and hope that a table is available when it's ready for pick-up.

HIGHLAND TAP
1026 North Highland Avenue NE
☎ 404-875-3673

A smoky, cozy joint where you will find the best martinis in Atlanta, served ice cold and perfectly dry.

KAYA
1068 Peachtree Street NE
☎ 404-733-5900

Expect the unexpected. The club boasts an impressive array of entertainment, from Latin music to drag shows to live bands. Especially hot are the Latin Nights on Saturdays. Merengue into the wee hours in an atmosphere that is *mucho caliente*.

After Dark

LEOPARD LOUNGE
84 12th Street NE
☎ 404-875-7562

The lounge is a stereotype for lounge lizards; pure cocktail culture.

LOCA LUNA
836 Juniper Street NE
☎ 404-875-4494

If you are searching for just the right spot to live "la vida loca" you've come to the right place. A spicy mix of dining, drinking and dancing.

MANUEL'S TAVERN
602 North Highland Avenue NE
☎ 404-526-3447

If you're searching for a politician or journalist after hours, this is the place to look. You'll find them munching away on exceptional burgers. It's the best place to search for intelligent life forms.

MARTINI CLUB
1140 Crescent Avenue NE
☎ 404-873-0794

The perfect small dive. A renovated residence with bars upstairs and down, a cigar area, and a piano. The patio is perfect for whiling away a summer evening waiting for James Bond to appear.

NORTHSIDE TAVERN
1058 Howell Mill Road NW
☎ 404-874-8745

An authentic, if rough looking, honky-tonk near Georgia Tech. Only for the brave of heart.

PARK 75
Four Seasons Hotel
75 14th Street
☎ 404-881-9898

Upscale, swank, a trysting place par excellence. A nice touch are the drinks in sample sizes. Can't decide between a rusty nail, vodka collins or a Manhattan? Have all three served on a dessert tray.

THE SHARK BAR AND RESTAURANT
571 Peachtree Street NE
☎ 404-815-8333

Happy hour is a happening at this trendy Peachtree bar. Floor to ceiling windows substitute for a patio.

VORTEX
878 Peachtree Street
☎ 404-875-1667

Vortex has overall the best liquor selection with more than 80 single malt Scotch varieties, 40 vodkas, 42 tequilas, 24 rums, 29 bourbons, nine different kinds of port and over 300 brands of beer. This could take a long time. You'll find a young, student crowd in evidence. The exceptionally good burgers are a delight.

After Dark

Buckhead

For nightlife in Atlanta, Buckhead is your best bet. There are more bars, discos, pickup joints, exotic dance emporiums, restaurants and cafés than you could ever hope to visit in one trip.

ASTI'S TERRACE LOUNGE
3199 Paces Ferry Place NW
☎ 404-364-9160

A cozy little club, attached to Asti's Italian restaurant, featuring jazz and Latin music. Perfect for a night out with your sweetheart.

BAR
250 E. Paces Ferry Road
☎ 404-841-0033

No theme. No attitude. Just Bar. Try a "bobsled shooter," which is poured through an ice sculpture. Open Wednesday through Saturday.

THE CHILI PEPPER
208 Pharr Road NE
☎ 404-812-9266

This high-energy dance club features a rooftop terrace. Raucous and a little bit raunchy.

COBALT
265 East Paces Ferry Road NE
☎ 404-760-9250

This beautifully designed discotheque/lounge features a two-level dance floor. Sleek interiors, and diverse music make it memorable.

DANTE'S DOWN THE HATCH
3380 Peachtree Road NE
☎ 404-266-1600

Imagine a pirate ship docked at a European village, complete with a moat and alligators. Okay, it's a little over the top, but the jazz trio is quite good and so is the featured fondue.

HAVE A NICE DAY CAFE
309 Peachtree Road NE
☎ 404-261-8898

Don't let the bright yellow smiley-face prevent you from entering. Inside you'll dance to the best of the '70s Music, from Wednesdays to Saturdays.

JELLYROLL'S
295 E. Paces Ferry Road
☎ 404-261-6864

Dueling pianos belt out the hits of yesterday and today. The waitstaff and audience participate in the singing and dancing. Jellyroll's is open from Wednesday through Saturday nights. Small cover charge.

JOHNNY'S HIDEAWAY
3771 Roswell Road NE
☎ 404-233-8026

You almost expect Frank Sinatra to come out and croon. This is one of Atlanta's favorite dance spots, where you can hear music from the '40s to the '80s.

LIQUID
293 Pharr Road NE
☎ 404-262-0604

A diverse, and very well dressed, 30s-and-up crowd inhabits this tri-level dance club, which offers live jazz and recorded R&B sounds.

OTTO'S
265 E. Paces Ferry Road
☎ 404-233-1133

Sleek, upscale, chic and trendy. You'll find live music downstairs and taped music upstairs. Otto's is in the epicenter of Buckhead's nightclub row, so don't

After Dark

expect to find parking. Save your ripped jeans for elsewhere; this club enforces a casually elegant dress code.

PARADOX
220 Pharr Road NE
☎ 404-760-1975

Perched above the Café Tu Tu Tango, this wrap-around deck with wide picture windows will give you a bird's-eye view of the restaurant below.

SANCTUARY
128 East Andrews Drive NE
☎ 404-262-1377

One of the hottest Latin dance nightclubs in Atlanta.

TONGUE & GROOVE
3055 Peachtree Road NE
☎ 404-261-2325

The velvet ropes outside the doors are a touch over the top for this eclectic drinking, dancing and lounging place. But this is, after all, Buckhead.

THE BAR AT THE PALM
3391 Peachtree Road NE, in the Swissôtel
☎ 404-814-1955

A place to relax, not snooty or too plush, despite its location. Here the bartender takes pride in saying, "Hey, I just run a saloon."

THE BAR AT THE RITZ-CARLTON
3434 Peachtree Road NE
☎ 404-237-2700

Nobody does it better. It's plush, and quiet, with cloth cocktail napkins and impeccable service. A woman waiting solo would be quite comfortable.

Marietta

RAY'S ON THE RIVER
6700 Powers Ferry Road SE
☎ 770-955-1187

You'll find light, contemporary jazz at this upscale eatery overlooking the Chattahoochee River. This is where Atlanta heads for Sunday brunch.

After Dark

Best Places To Stay

Atlanta is one of the three top cities in the US for convention destinations, and as such has a prodigious number of hotel rooms for a city its size. The compact downtown area alone has more than 10,000 rooms. Even so, to get the space you desire, be sure to book well in advance, as conventions fill those hotel rooms quickly at all times of the year.

But Atlanta hotels are perfect for weekend getaways. In general, the convention and trade show people take Friday flights home, leaving lots of rooms available at exceptionally good rates. If you want to indulge in the good life at a four-star hotel, Atlanta on a weekend is a good place to do so.

Almost invariably, you'll find a major hotel close to either the freeways or MARTA transportation, making it very easy to get around the city. Be sure to consider how close your hotel is to what you wish to explore in order to save precious sightseeing hours. If you want to shop till you drop, then the hotels around Lenox Square are a good choice. Ready to cheer on your favorite team? Then Downtown is for you. A weekend with the arts? Midtown is your best bet. And for all-around fun of shopping, dining, dancing and a taste of nightlife you'll want to be Buckhead bound.

The Alive price scale for accommodations is based on the rate for a double room, per night.

ACCOMMODATIONS PRICE SCALE
Inexpensive . . . . $50-$100
Moderate . . . . $100-$150
Expensive. . . . . $150-$200
Deluxe . . . . .More than $200

Downtown

ATLANTA HILTON AND TOWERS
255 Cortland Street
Atlanta, Georgia 30303
☎ 404-659-2000, www.atlanta.hilton.com
Expensive-Deluxe

One of the city's largest hotels (it occupies an entire city block), and a convention favorite, this hotel has fairly standard rooms. There are more luxurious accommodations available in the Tower. You'll find five restaurants on site, including Trader Vic's and Nikolai's Roof, an Atlanta favorite for special occasions.

ATLANTA MARRIOTT MARQUIS
265 Peachtree Center Avenue
Atlanta, GA 30303
☎ 404-521-0000, www.marriott.com/marriott/atlmq
Deluxe

This is the South's largest-capacity hotel. It is connected to the shops of Peachtree Center by a skywalk, and is another conventioneers favorite. The unusual atrium lobby, designed by John Portman, soars for an amazing 48 stories. The rooms are of average size and were redecorated in 1997.

HYATT REGENCY ATLANTA
265 Peachtree Street
Atlanta, Georgia 30303
☎ 404-577-1234, 800-233-1234, www.hyatt.com
Deluxe

Another John Portman creation, the Hyatt Regency launched the "atrium look" in 1967. The blue bubble dome atop the Polaris restaurant makes the hotel readily identifiable in the Atlanta skyline. The rooms are very comfortably furnished, and amenities on site include a pool, health club, and business services.

OMNI HOTEL AT THE CNN CENTER
100 CNN Center
Atlanta, GA 30335
☎ 404-659-0000, www.omnihotelcnn.com
Expensive-Deluxe

Right beside the CNN center, and across the street from the World Congress Center, this hotel is a popular choice with conventions. Its lobby is eclectic, combining old world charm with contemporary accents. The rooms are large and comfortable.

RITZ-CARLTON ATLANTA
181 Peachtree Street NE
Atlanta, GA 30303
☎ 404-659-0400, www.ritzcarlton.com
Expensive-Deluxe

A touch of the old world in downtown Atlanta. A 17th-century Flemish tapestry adorns the Peachtree Street entry, and afternoon tea is served in the lobby. Contemporary touches include The City Grill, a new restaurant with a veranda that juts out above the street level. Spacious guest rooms are appointed with plump sofas and writing tables. Some of the suites have four-poster beds. It's the Ritz, so don't forget to leave your shoes out for a complimentary polish.

SHERATON ATLANTA
165 Courtland Street
Atlanta, GA 30303
☎ 404-659-6500, 800-833-8624 or 800-325-3535
Expensive

Just one block away from Peachtree Center, the hotel features an indoor pool, business center and a fully equipped health center. Designed for the business traveler, it has abundant meeting spaces and two-level hospitality suites for entertaining.

WESTIN PEACHTREE PLAZA
210 Peachtree Street NW
Atlanta, GA 30303
☎ 404-659-1400, www.westin.com
Expensive

The landmark cylinder shape, designed by John Portman, makes this hotel easy to find in the Atlanta skyline. Pie-shaped rooms are decorated in pastel hues and dark woods. The Sun Dial, the revolving restaurant 70 stories high, atop the hotel, has great views – particularly dramatic with an approaching thunderstorm.

SUITE HOTEL UNDERGROUND ATLANTA
54 Peachtree Street, at Upper Alabama
Atlanta, Georgia 30303
☎ 404-223-5555
Inexpensive-Moderate

An unassuming little hotel overlooking Underground Atlanta, it almost goes unnoticed by those passing by. Created from a 19th-century structure, with several stories added later, the hotel has small suites decorated with traditional furniture and contemporary prints.

BEST WESTERN INN AT THE PEACHTREES
330 West Peachtree Street, NW
Atlanta, GA 30308
☎ 404-577-6970, 800-242-4642 or 800-937-8376
Inexpensive-Moderate

Modest and unassuming, this is a good deal in a good location for the convention attendee.

DAYS INN DOWNTOWN
300 Spring Street
Atlanta, Georgia 30308
☎ 404-523-1144, 800-DAYS INN (329-7466)
Moderate-Expensive

Located across the street from the Apparel, Inforum and Merchandise Mart, this 263 room hotel has cable TV and an outdoor pool. Bring the family, kids under 17 stay free.

Midtown

THE FOUR SEASONS
75 14th Street
Atlanta, GA 30309
☎ 404-881-9898
Deluxe

The most opulent hotel in Midtown, and one of the most luxurious in Atlanta, this hotel occupies only the first 19 floors of a 53-story skyscraper. The remaining floors are occupied by offices and private residences. Guest rooms feature original artwork, mini-bars, and marble bathrooms with hair dryers and robes.

MARRIOTT SUITES ATLANTA MIDTOWN
35 14th Street
Atlanta, GA 30309
☎ 404-876-8888
Expensive-Deluxe

Featuring generously proportioned suites in pastel colors, it's an excellent location for a weekend of museum hopping and theater or symphony in Midtown.

ATLANTA RENAISSANCE
590 W. Peachtree Street
Atlanta, GA 30308
☎ 404-881-6000 or 800-468-3571
Expensive

Halfway between Downtown and Midtown, this 25-story hotel has eye-popping views of the skyline. The rooms are large with private balconies. Deluxe Club Level suites have private lounges and concierge service.

MARRIOTT RESIDENCE INN MIDTOWN
1041 W. Peachtree Street
☎ 404-607-1112, 800-331-3131
Expensive

Just one block from the MARTA Midtown Station, this seven-story, suites-only hotel is an excellent location for those on business or leisure travel. Free continental breakfast is served in a room off the lobby.

WYNDHAM HOTEL MIDTOWN
12510th Street NE
Atlanta, GA 30309
☎ 404-873-4800, 800-WYNDHAM (996-3426)
www.wyndham.com
Moderate-Expensive

Spacious rooms are highlighted by bay windows, armchairs with hassocks, televisions and coffee makers. The Executive King rooms include a sofa, extra television and telephones. Two blocks from the MARTA Midtown Station.

SHERATON COLONY SQUARE
188 14th Street NE
Atlanta, GA 30361
☎ 404-892-6000, 800-325-3535
Inexpensive-Moderate

An excellent location for theater, arts and symphony expeditions, only a block away from the Woodruff Arts Center. In fact, you barely need to walk that far, with the 14th Street Playhouse just across the street. The rooms are large with contemporary furnishings. Rooms on higher floors have very nice views of the city.

Best Places to Stay

GEORGIAN TERRACE HOTEL
659 Peachtree Street
Atlanta, Georgia 30308
☎ 404-897-1991
Expensive

Just across the street from the Fox Theatre, this is
an intriguing hotel that began life as an apartment
building. In 1939, the cast of *Gone With the Wind*
stayed here for the film's premiere. The rooms are
quite large and well furnished but the amenities
need some work, and it would benefit from a better
restaurant. Located two blocks from the MARTA
North Avenue Station.

ANSLEY INN
253 15 Street NE
Atlanta, Georgia 30309
☎ 404-872-9000
Moderate

This charming bed-and-breakfast, nestled in the confusion that is Ansley Park, is a delight. The hotel is
housed in a beautifully restored English Tudor-style
mansion, filled with paintings, chandeliers and quality antiques. Each guest room has a Jacuzzi in addition to private bath, and boasts a fireplace as well.

GRANADA SUITES HOTEL
1302 West Peachtree Street
Atlanta, Georgia 30309
☎ 404-876-6100
Moderate

Built in 1924, the Granada has a quaint Spanish Co-
lonial-style that is unusual for Atlanta. It began life
as an apartment building, and was converted in
1986 to an all-suite hotel. Across the street from the

MARTA Arts Center station, it's in a great location for either weekend or business travel.

HAMPTON INN MIDTOWN
1152 Spring Street
Atlanta, GA 30309
☎ 404-872-3234, 800-HAMPTON (426-7866)
Inexpensive

Well-placed budget hotel in a location that makes both Downtown and Midtown business sites easily accessible. Good facilities for small meetings.

Buckhead

GRAND HYATT BUCKHEAD
3300 Peachtree Road NE
Atlanta, GA 30305
☎ 404-365-8100, 800-233-1234, www.hyatt.com
Expensive-Deluxe

A 35-foot waterfall and a 9,000-square-foot Japanese garden are highlights of this modern hotel. Originally a Nikko Hotel, the Oriental influence is still evident in the understated décor of black, gray and purple. High-quality Japanese art adorns the walls of both public and private rooms. The rooms themselves are quite spacious, and more American than Japanese. A really great feature of this hotel is the complimentary shuttle, which will take guests anywhere within a two-mile radius. For Buckhead dining and shopping this is a real plus.

Best Places to Stay

RITZ-CARLTON BUCKHEAD
3434 Peachtree Road NE
Atlanta, GA 30326
☎ 404-237-2700, www.ritzcarlton.com
Expensive-Deluxe

This elegant retreat offers deluxe accommodations in a quiet, understated fashion. The rooms are a bit small, but beautifully furnished. You'll feel as if you were in Europe rather than across the street from Lenox Square. The Dining Room Restaurant has won many awards, but it captures hearts for the cozy bar and dance floor just a few romantic steps away.

SWISSOTEL
3391 Peachtree Road NE
Atlanta, GA 30326
☎ 404-365-0065
Expensive-Deluxe

Swissôtel's sleek exterior belies its European heart. This chic glass-and-white-enamel exterior echoes the façade of the High Museum of Art. The rooms are huge, and furnished in the Biedermeier style in shades of gray and lavender. The bathrooms are large enough to hold a hockey game. This hotel is a favorite with business travelers for its in-room fax machines, and large desks with good lighting.

JW MARRIOTT
3300 Lenox Road NE
Atlanta, Georgia 30326
☎ 404-262-3344
Expensive-Deluxe

This handsome hotel features Chippendale-style furniture in the lobby and guest rooms. The hotel connects directly to Lenox Square Mall, making it the perfect location for serious shoppers. The guest rooms are large, and have generously sized bathrooms with separate shower stalls.

HOLIDAY INN BUCKHEAD
3377 Peachtree Road NE
Atlanta, Georgia 30326
☎ 404-264-1111, 800-535-0707
Moderate

The best location for serious shopping expeditions, this hotel is beside Lenox Square and just south of Phipps Plaza. Rooms include cable TV, modem hook-ups and coffee makers. The MARTA Lenox Station is a moderate walk away.

EMBASSY SUITES HOTEL BUCKHEAD
3285 Peachtree Road NE
Atlanta, Georgia 30305
☎ 404-261-7733, 800-EMBASSY (362-2779)
Expensive-Deluxe

This contemporary hotel, only a few blocks north of Phipps Plaza and Lenox Square, offers a range of suites from basic to ultra-deluxe. A good location for Oglethorpe University.

RESIDENCE INN BY MARRIOTT
2960 Piedmont Road SE
☎ 404-239-0677, 800-331-3131
Moderate

If you have come to Buckhead to sample the cuisine, this location is an ideal one, close to both the Buckhead Diner and Pricci (see the Buckhead section of *Best Places to Eat*, pages 176 and 184). Suites have fully equipped kitchens; most have curbside parking and a private entrance. The hotel has a health club and a pool.

SHERATON BUCKHEAD HOTEL
3405 Lenox Road NE
Atlanta, Georgia 30326
☎ 404-261-9250, 800-325-3535
Moderate-Expensive

A convention and business hotel in the heart of Buckhead. The hotel has a somewhat sprawling design that makes getting from the lobby to the far reaches a bit of a challenge. Good, if uninspiring room décor and service.

WYNDHAM GARDEN
3340 Peachtree Road
Atlanta, GA 30326
☎ 404-23-1234, 800-WYNDHAM (996-3426)
www.wyndham.com
Moderate

Reasonable rates, good-sized rooms and a prime location (near both Phipps Plaza and Lenox Square) earn high marks for this hotel. The service and ambiance don't compare with its ritzy neighbors, but this is a good value.

LENOX INN
3387 Lenox Road
Atlanta, GA 30326
☎ 404-261-5500
Inexpensive-Moderate

Spread among four buildings, which are two and three-stories high, this will remind you more of a motel. The rooms are nicely decorated in tones of cream and forest green. This is a good value for the location, but don't expect too much.

Northwest Atlanta

RENAISSANCE WAVERLY HOTEL
2450 Galleria Parkway
Atlanta, GA 30339
☎ 770-953-4500; www.renaissance hotels.com
Deluxe

Located near the Galleria Mall and about 10 minutes from Buckhead, this is one of Atlanta's most deluxe properties. The rooms are outfitted in rich autumn hues and 19th-century English reproduction mahogany furniture. Don't stay here if a view is a high priority; the rooms overlook I-285. It's an oasis in the wilderness of business towers.

WYNDHAM AT VININGS
2857 Paces Ferry Road
Atlanta, GA 30339
☎ 770-432-5555, 800-WYNDHAM
www.wyndham.com
Expensive

In a park-like setting in the upscale suburb of Vinings, this hotel is convenient to the major business districts and Cumberland Mall. The rooms are quite spacious and comfortably furnished. The tennis courts are a bonus for fitness fans.

Decatur Area

EMORY INN
1641 Clifton Road
Atlanta, GA 30329
☎ 404-712-6700
Moderate

One of the best-kept secrets in Atlanta is this hotel adjacent to Emory University Conference Center in the Druid Hills neighborhood. Nearly everyone who comes to Emory tries to stay here if there is a vacancy. Nestled in a forest-like area, this hotel provides a peaceful retreat from the hustle and bustle of Downtown. But, it's near enough to Midtown (three miles) and Downtown (five miles) to be convenient. The inn is furnished in early American pine furniture.

HOLIDAY INN SELECT DECATUR
130 Clairmont Avenue
Decatur, GA
☎ 404-371-0204, 800-535-0707
Moderate

The nearby Decatur MARTA station makes getting to and from this hotel as easy as can be. This 185-room charmer pampers its guests with amenities that include copies of *USA Today*, in-room hair dryers, coffee makers, irons and ironing board, plus free transportation within a five-mile radius.

Airport Area

HILTON ATLANTA AIRPORT
1031 Virginia Avenue
Atlanta, GA 30354
☎ 404-767-9000
Expensive

A complete conference center close to the airport. The standard size rooms have data ports and the latest in voice messaging. If you are a sports fan, you'll revel in the Finish Line Sports Bar, complete with a stock car suspended from the ceiling.

CLUB HOTEL BY DOUBLETREE
5010 Old National Highway
☎ 404-761-4000, 800-222-TREE (8733)
Moderate

Just outside the Perimeter and south of Hartsfield Atlanta International Airport, the Club Hotel offers a shuttle pick up service, complimentary coffee and a copy of *USA Today*. An indoor/outdoor pool and conference center complete the amenities.

Best Places to Eat

If you arrive in Atlanta expecting to find only barbecue served up with greens, black-eyed peas and grits, you'll be pleasantly surprised. Atlanta has restaurants that rival those in the largest and most cosmopolitan cities.

Depending on what you are in the mood for, you can dress to the nines and go wild with your expense account at fine dining establishments, or be as casual as you like and spend only a modest amount.

Atlanta's increasingly diverse ethnic communities have added a much-needed foreign flair to the local palate. You'll find almost every type of food imaginable, from dim sum to Cuban sandwiches, Moroccan couscous to California rolls.

Eastside, westside, all around the town, Atlantans will go almost any distance for a new and trendy restaurant. So be prepared to drive a little off the beaten path, or at least off Peachtree, to find some of these culinary delights.

Keep in mind that restaurants open and close all the time in Atlanta, but the list is up-to-date as we go to press.

DINING PRICE SCALE
Price scale reflects the cost of an average entrée.
Inexpensive . . . . $5-$10
Moderate . . . . $10-$25
Expensive. . . . . $25-$50
Deluxe . . . . .More than $50

Downtown

American

DAILEY'S RESTAURANT
17 International Boulevard
☎ 404-681-3303
Moderate

This restored warehouse has an intimate, clubby atmosphere with lots of wood and low-key lighting. Huge portions and a dessert bar to die for are hallmarks of this Atlanta favorite. Dailey's is open Mondays-Fridays for lunch and dinner, Saturdays and Sundays for dinner only; expect a long wait at peak times.

MUMBO JUMBO BAR/GRILL
89 Park Place NE
☎ 404-523-0330
Moderate

Mumbo Jumbo is a trendy restaurant with food by Michelin star Chef Guenter Seeger and Head Chef

Dean Max. It's also one of the top night spots in the Downtown area (see *After Dark*, page 133).

Asian

HSU'S GOURMET
192 Peachtree Center Avenue NE
☎ 404-659-2788
Moderate

The sumptuous décor, reminiscent of a shrine or temple, belies the cranky service. Not your run-of-the-mill Chinese fare. Try the dry-fried string beans, or the caramelized pieces of pork. Hsu's is open daily for lunch and dinner, and on Saturdays and Sundays for dinner only.

PACIFIC RIM BISTRO
303 Peachtree Street NE
☎ 404-893-0018
Moderate

Very popular restaurant with the downtown lunch crowd on weekdays, and offering a full and varied Asian dinner menu daily. The oysters steamed in black bean sauce are outstanding, as is the sushi.

Bars & Pubs

MAX LAGER'S AMERICAN GRILL & BREWERY
320 Peachtree St.
☎ 404-525-4400
Moderate

Freshly brewed beer, grilled steaks and wood-fired pizza, for lunch and dinner daily. Need we say more?

Barbecue

HAROLD'S BARBECUE
171 McDonough Blvd. SE
☎ 404-627-9268
Inexpensive

A typical barbecue joint featuring the best Brunswick stew and cracklin' bread in town. Harold's is open for lunch and dinner, Mondays-Saturdays.

Brunch

SYLVIA'S
241 Central Avenue Southwest
☎ 404-529-9692
Expensive

Barbecued pork ribs, sweet and sour chicken, fried fish and peach cobbler. Add unlimited mimosas and bloody Marys, top it off with gospel music, and you have the recipe for an outstanding brunch experience.

Continental

ATLANTA GRILL
181 Peachtree Street NE, in the Ritz-Carlton Hotel, Buckhead
☎ 404-659-0400
Deluxe

Perched above Peachtree Street, this restaurant has an open-air veranda that's perfect for people watching. The restaurant features contemporary Southern with a New Orleans-French Quarter flavor. This has become one of Atlanta's newest gathering places downtown. Splurge on the filet of grilled salmon or a New York strip steak, and add peeled asparagus spears or macaroni and cheese (yes, macaroni and cheese) to complete the meal.

NIKOLAI'S ROOF
255 Courtland Street in the Atlanta Hilton
☎ 404-221-6362
Expensive-Deluxe

When you need to feel like a Russian csar or csarina, grab your ermine tails and ascend to Nikolai's Roof. The view alone is worth the pricey prix fixe menu which varies with the availability and seasonality of game.

Lunch Spots

ROSA'S PIZZA
62 Broad Street
☎ 404-521-2596
Inexpensive

Rosa's serves the only New York-style pizza in Atlanta. Very popular hole-in-the-wall eatery. Two slices with one topping and drink are under $5. They also serve calzone, hot subs, and sausage rolls. Seating is available downstairs in the University of Georgia common room; open Mondays-Fridays, 11-6.

HONG KONG DRAGON
131 Cone Street
☎ 404-584-8676
Inexpensive

West Coast Chinese buffet with great egg drop soup and some very spicy selections. Open for lunch only,

Downtown lunch spots fill quickly at noon. If you want to be seated promptly it's best to arrive before 11:30 am or after 1:30 pm.

Mondays-Fridays; the menu is all you can eat and drink for $6.

MAMA NINFA'S
231 Peachtree Street NE
☎ 404-521-3500
Inexpensive-Moderate

Best Tex-Mex in the downtown area. Fresh tortilla chips made on site. Try the enchiladas or fajitas; Mama Ninfa's is open daily for lunch and dinner.

CARNEGIE'S DOWNTOWN
55 Park Place NE
☎ 404-588-0332
Inexpensive-Moderate

Slightly upscale, this is where the lawyers hang out. Good daily specials. The tuna melt is highly recommended. Carnegie's is open for lunch and dinner, Mondays-Fridays.

Mexican

MAMA NINFA'S
231 Peachtree Street
☎ 404-521-3500
Inexpensive

Yes, it is part of a chain, but it's good! Handmade tortillas, sizzling fajitas, camarones, enchiladas and frozen "Ninfarita" top off the meal. Mama Ninfa's is open daily for lunch and dinner.

Pizza

FELLINI'S PIZZA
Inexpensive

Fellini's is a local favorite; it is a prolific chain of small but good restaurants. You will see them in multiple locations in the city, from Downtown/Midtown to the outlying areas. Try the selections by the slice.

Seafood

SAVANNAH FISH COMPANY
Westin Peachtree Hotel
Peachtree St., and International Blvd.
☎ 404-589-7476
Expensive

This fish house serves food with a southern accent and lots of panache, such as smashed red potatoes and fried green tomatoes.

Nibble on lavosh and a smoked fish terrine at Savannah Fish Company while waiting for your entrée to arrive. Perfection.

Southern

PITTYPAT'S PORCH
25 International Boulevard
☎ 404-525-8228
Moderate-Expensive

Pittypat was Scarlett's scatterbrained auntie in *Gone With the Wind*, but you'll find nothing "flaky" about this renowned eatery. Since it opened in 1967, it's been serving up "Twelve Oaks Barbecue," sweet potato pie, and peach cobbler with Southern hospitality. Okay, it's touristy and a little over-priced, but if you're determined to seek out Scarlett, this is a good place to gain sustenance during your search.

SYLVIA'S
241 Central Avenue Southwest
☎ 404-529-9692
Expensive

Sylvia's is known for barbecued pork ribs, sweet and sour chicken, fried fish and peach cobbler. They are also open for brunch on Sundays.

Steak

SUN DIAL RESTAURANT BAR & VIEW
72nd Floor of the Westin Peachtree Plaza
Peachtree at International Boulevard
☎ 404-589-7506
Expensive

A steakhouse above the rest with an extraordinary view. It is traditional to come here at sunset, but in a thunderstorm the view can be truly spectacular. Don't miss the bucket of shrimp appetizer. Sun Dial is open daily for lunch and dinner.

Midtown

American

AGNES & MURIEL'S
1514 Monroe Drive NE
☎ 404-885-1000
Inexpensive-Moderate

Imagine a '50s diner in a refurbished brick home on the edge of Ansley Park. This is where you go for comfort food – meatloaf, honey-battered fried chicken and greens. Very down home. Open daily for lunch and dinner, Saturdays and Sundays for brunch.

THE PLEASANT PEASANT
555 Peachtree Street NE
☎ 404-874-3223
Expensive

This Atlanta mainstay features mammoth salads at lunch and contemporary cuisine specials in the evening. Appetizers range from crab cakes to marinated goat cheese. The black bean soup is a house specialty. For dinner, try the pepper-crusted New York strip. Lunch and dinner are served daily; dinner only on Saturdays and Sundays. Reservations are accepted, and there is valet parking.

Asian

NICKIEMOTO'S
990 Piedmont Avenue NE
☎ 404-253-2010
Moderate-Expensive

Sushi and Asian fusion come together at this trendy spot. The wait staff is very knowledgeable and helpful. This is a vibrant but noisy place to have lunch or dinner, and the wooden booths and tiny tables don't make for the most comfortable seating. But the place is always packed because the food is so good. Try the catfish with ginger or the tuna rolled in a peppercorn crust. Nickiemoto's is open daily.

TAMARIND THAI CUISINE
88 14th Street NW
☎ 404-873-4888
Expensive

This little Midtown gem will put a dent in your wallet, but you won't mind; the flavors are vibrant, the presentations artful, and service is terrific. Try it for lunch during the week; dinner is served daily.

Bars & Pubs

GORDON BIERSCH BREW PUB
848 Peachtree Street
☎ 404-870-0805
Moderate

A beer sampler is a nice touch at this aging yuppie hangout. Pastas, stir fry and oh-so-trendy bar foods. This Midtown location is just like all the others in the chain and just as noisy; they are open daily for lunch and dinner until 11 pm.

JOE'S ON JUNIPER
1049 Juniper Street NE
☎ 404-875-6634
Inexpensive-Moderate

Outstanding selection of beers from around the world, any one of which will complement chicken with queso nachos, spicy chili, and terrific burgers. A party atmosphere prevails in this mostly gay pub, open Mondays-Saturdays from 11 am-2 am, and Sundays from 11 am to midnight.

PRINCE OF WALES
1144 Piedmont Avenue
☎ 404-876-0227
Inexpensive-Moderate

Lovely pub with a patio; when the sun shines, you would swear you were having a pint at a pub in the English countryside. Just across the street from Piedmont Park. The Prince of Wales is open daily and serves good bar food in the best tradition of British bites, but beware the jalapeño tartar sauce with the fish and chips.

Barbecue

FAT MATT'S RIB SHACK
1811 Piedmont Avenue
☎ 404-607-1622
Inexpensive-Moderate

Perhaps the best pulled-pork sandwiches in the city. Expect to wait in line to place your order, then be ready to dive for the nearest available table. Great

jazz in the evenings, good food for lunch and dinner
daily.

Bistros

EINSTEIN'S
1077 Juniper Street
☎ 404-876-7925
Moderate

One of Midtown's nicest outdoor eateries, Einstein's
is open daily for lunch and dinner. The puns on the
menu are almost as delicious as the food itself. Try
the Quantum Catch (catch of the day), or a Massive
Salad, the Einstein Grille or the Three Cheese The-
ory. A good choice for starry nights so you can con-
template the universe.

Brunch

HUEY'S
1816 Peachtree Road NW
☎ 404-873-2037
Inexpensive

A New Orleans-style café, complete with beignets at
breakfast and brunch. Truly a down-home choles-
terol fest, Huey's also serves lunch and dinner.

JAVA JIVE
790 Ponce de Leon Avenue NE
☎ 404-876-6161
Inexpensive

The gingerbread waffle, served only on the weekends, is worth the trip. The 40s retro-style eatery is
authentic, right down to the swing music on the ra-

dio. Java Jive serves breakfast only, Tuesdays-Sundays.

Cajun & Creole

FRENCH QUARTER FOOD SHOP
923 Peachtree Street NE
☎ 404-875-2409
Inexpensive-Moderate

This restaurant is a favorite with the Fox Theatre crowd, so be prepared for a wait on performance nights. Open for lunch and dinner Mondays-Saturdays,with good music, cold beer and just the right amount of smoky spice in every entrée.

Caribbean & Cuban

BRIDGETOWN GRILL
689 Peachtree St., NE
☎ 404-873-5361
Inexpensive-Moderate

A taste of the Caribbean in downtown Atlanta, this has become Atlanta's favorite Jamaican restaurant. Upbeat, colorful and really good food served to the accompaniment of Reggae music in the background. The jerk chicken, reggae ribs and chipotle shrimp sauté are all worth a try. Great place to have a meal before or after a show at the Fox Theatre.

Try the couch potatoes at Bridgetown Grill, a mountain of steak fries topped with black bean chili, melted jack cheese and sliced jalapeños.

LAS PALMERAS
368 Fifth Street NE near GA Tech
☎ 404-872-0846
Inexpensive

The black beans and Cuban sandwiches are always dependably good.

Continental

THE ABBEY
163 Ponce de Leon at Piedmont
☎ 404-876-8532
Expensive

A harpist in The Abbey's choir loft adds a heavenly touch.

Within a restored church, you'll be served by waiters dressed as monks, in soft candlelit surroundings. A favorite for celebratory occasions, it's undeniably touristy, but fun. There is always a vegetarian entrée on the menu.

BACCHANALIA
1198 Howell Mill Road
☎ 404-365-4010
Deluxe

Bacchanalia will surprise you with its industrial funk location and its solemn, yet superb, service. The food is voluptuous. Caviar eaten with a mother-of-pearl spoon, melting beef short ribs over satiny potatoes, and decadent chocolate cake. Dinner is a prix-fixe menu currently at $55 per person, and worth every penny; Bacchanalia also serves lunch, and they are open Tuesdays-Saturdays.

THE MANSION
179 Ponce de Leon Avenue
☎ 404-876-0727
Moderate-Expensive

Gracious living in the South. Aptly named, the restaurant is housed in a grand, 1885 home perched atop a hill. Very dressy, this is a popular spot for weddings and special occasions. Start your meal with an appetizer such as steamed lobster with wilted lettuce, or lobster bisque. For the entrée, try the beef Wellington or potato-crusted snapper.

French

LE SAINT AMOUR
1620 Piedmont Road NE
☎ 404-881-0300
Deluxe

Authentic French food in a location that seems to have been transplanted from a village in the French wine country. Try the sole meunière, or the filet mignon.

Indian

TOUCH OF INDIA
962 Peachtree Street NE
☎ 404-876-7777
Moderate

This is one of Atlanta's oldest Indian restaurants, distinctively painted with the green, orange and white colors of the Indian flag. The tandoori dishes are mouth watering, and you'll find many vegetarian entrées, too.

Italian

VENI, VIDI, VICI
41 14th Street NE
☎ 404-875-8424
Moderate

Too much to eat? Next door to Veni, Vidi, Vici is a bocce court where you can work off a few calories.

Northern Italian cuisine in the heart of Midtown. Roast suckling pig, buffalo milk ricotta-filled tortellini, and a slice of whole roasted salmon are but a few of the items on the menu. Veni, Vidi, Vici serves dinner daily, and is open for lunch Mondays-Fridays.

Mexican & Southwestern

ZOCALO'S
187 10th Street NE
☎ 404-249-7576
Inexpensive-Moderate

This restaurant offers a serious menu of specialty dishes, prepared with an attention to detail that is unmatched in any other Mexican restaurant in the city. Its cozy patio is a lovely place to lunch. The owners boast of the largest tequila selection in the city.

Moroccan

IMPERIAL FEZ
2285 Peachtree Road
☎ 404-351-0870
Expensive

Cross the threshold into Morocco! A long-time Atlanta favorite for celebrations of any sort, the Imperial Fez is great fun, not haute cuisine. The atmosphere is friendly, and the physical surroundings are dark enough to make you ask for a flashlight to read the menu. This is something to do once every thousand-and-one nights.

Pizza

ROCKY'S BRICK OVEN
1770 Peachtree Street NW
☎ 404-876-1111
Inexpensive-Moderate

The best of the thin-crust pizzas to be found in the city. Try the white and Margarita varieties.

Southern

MARY MAC'S TEA ROOM
224 Ponce de Leon Avenue
☎ 404-876-1800
Moderate

"Fried green tomatoes" is more than just the name of a book, and this is the place to sample them in the city. Atlantans take great pride in the hearty, regional cuisine offered here. Hillary Rodham Clinton lunched here while on a visit.

Buckhead

American

ANTHONY'S
3109 Piedmont Avenue
☎ 404-262-7379
Moderate-Expensive

One of the restaurants Scarlett would have on her top ten list of ways never to go hungry again. This is a romantic, restored 1797 plantation home in yuppie central Buckhead. Dine in one of 12 beautifully decorated rooms, on fare that ranges from filet mignon to fish. Open for dinner, Mondays-Saturdays.

BUCKHEAD DINER
3073 Piedmont Road
☎ 404-262-3336
Expensive

The Buckhead Diner was the model for the diner in Euro-Disney.

The Buckhead Diner is one of the best places for people and car watching, and the best place to have dinner solo. Creative American cuisine served in an energetic environment. Crisped soft shell crabs and jalapeño coleslaw are some of the innovative offerings.

The restaurant is open seven days a week for lunch and dinner, but be prepared for a wait on any one of those days. Brunch is particularly popular on Sundays. Go early if you don't require an eye-opener, which cannot be served until noon.

PANO'S & PAUL'S
1232 West Paces Ferry Road
☎ 404-261-3662
Deluxe

This restaurant sets the standard for luxury dining in Atlanta. Creative American cuisine has netted this Atlanta favorite Mobil's 4-Star rating and *Gourmet Magazine*'s choice for Atlanta's Best. The atmosphere is opulent, with an old world flavor. Fried lobster tail with honey-mustard dressing and smoked salmon in rice paper are two menu favorites. Pano's & Paul's is open for dinner Mondays-Saturdays.

Asian

CHOPSTIX
4279 Roswell Road NE
☎ 404-255-4868
Expensive

Try Chopstix for upscale Chinese food with creative entrées. Lamb tenderloin with hot pepper sauce and duck ravioli are just a sample of what waits inside. Lunch and dinner are served daily; dinner only on Saturdays and Sundays.

SOTO JAPANESE RESTAURANT
3330 Piedmont Road NE
☎ 404-233-2005
Moderate

Some say it's the best sushi bar in town. You can count on a good variety of cooked dishes as well. Soto serves dinner only, Mondays-Saturdays.

Bars & Pubs

FADO IRISH PUB
3035 Peachtree Road NE
☎ 404-841-0066
Inexpensive-Moderate

A little bit of the "old sod" transplanted to Buckhead, Fado is a lot of fun. It really looks like an Irish pub, with pints of Guinness, fish and chips, and breakfast that can only be described as a heart attack on a plate. The name "fado" means "once upon a time" (pronounce it as "FAH-dough," with the emphasis on the first syllable). Fado is open daily for lunch and dinner.

JOHN HARVARD'S BREW HOUSE
3039 Peachtree Road
☎ 404-816-2739
Moderate

New beers and a constantly changing menu keeps the locals coming back to this Buckhead location. John Harvard's serves lunch and dinner Sundays and Mondays from 11:30 am to midnight, Tuesdays-Thursdays from 11:30-1 am, and Fridays and Saturdays from 11:30-2 am.

ROCK BOTTOM
3242 Peachtree Road NE
☎ 404-264-0253
Moderate

This is not your average pub fare. Try the hot beer pretzels with mustard, or the brown ale chicken with mashed potatoes; they are open daily for lunch and dinner.

Barbecue

THE RIB RANCH
25 Irby Avenue NW
☎ 404-233-7644
Inexpensive

Just a little hole-in-the-wall eatery with Texas-style ribs; the Rib Ranch is open Sundays-Wednesdays, 11 am-10 pm, and Thursdays-Saturdays, 11 am-11 pm.

Bistros

TOM TOM: A BISTRO
3393 Peachtree Road, Lenox Square Mall
☎ 404-264-1163
Moderate

A fusion menu showcases the profusion of Asian, Mediterranean, Southwestern and French items on the menu. This place is open for lunch and dinner daily, and has something for everyone. Try the spinach ravioli or barbecued salmon.

Brunch

CORNER CAFE
3070 Piedmont Road NE
☎ 404-240-1978
Inexpensive-Moderate

This is where Atlanta goes for a power breakfast. Traditional eggs and bacon pair well with financial statements. The Corner Café also serves lunch daily and dinner on weeknights.

ORIGINAL PANCAKE HOUSE
4330 Peachtree Road NE
☎ 404-237-4116
Inexpensive

This is breakfast. Eggs, bacon, pancakes and syrup. Feeling adventurous? Try the giant Dutch apple pancake. The restaurant is open for breakfast, lunch and dinner.

Cajun & Creole

McKINNON'S OF LOUISIANE
3209 Maple Drive NE
☎ 404-237-1313
Expensive

There's not a Cajun staple missing from the list – from gumbo to oysters Rockefeller to blackened catfish. McKinnon's serves dinner only, and they are closed Sundays.

Continental

103 WEST
103 West Paces Ferry Road NW
☎ 404-233-5993
Deluxe

Stylish, ornate, and sometimes too busy. Specialties of the house include veal, batter-fried lobster tail, and venison so rich and tender you could consider taking out a hunting license. This is a place to celebrate – in style.

SEEGER'S
111 W. Paces Ferry Road NW
☎ 404-846-9779
Deluxe

Tuna tart with black truffles, Scottish deer medal-lions, scallops poached in beet juice and grapefruit terrine with goat yogurt sorbet are just a few of the innovative selections you can find on Seeger's menu. The restaurant is stylish and spare, just right for the types who also enjoy the ambience of the W Hotel (see page 219). Seeger's serves dinner only, Mon-days-Saturdays; reservations are required.

French

ANIS
2974 Grandview Avenue
☎ 404-233-9889
Expensive-Deluxe

The next best thing to visiting Provence itself. Drink chilled white wine and feast on mussels marinière, or a risotto to die for. The outdoor patio is wonderful on a summer evening. The restaurant is located on a formerly residential street in Buckhead that is now something of a restaurant row, but the quiet adds to the French countryside ambiance.

BRASSERIE LE COZE
3393 Peachtree Road NE, Lenox Square Mall
☎ 404-266-1440
Expensive

Forget that you found this restaurant in the largest mall in Atlanta. It's a lovingly reproduced Paris brasserie in the midst of Lenox Square. Try the skate wings browned in butter, a signature dish from the day the restaurant opened.

SOLEIL
3081 Maple Drive NE
☎ 404-467-1790
Moderate

Southern French fare, well executed and sensibly priced. Try the grilled Cornish hen or one of the excellent salads.

TOULOUSE
2293 Peachtree Road NE
☎ 404-351-9533
Expensive

A serious wine list and an unchanging menu of French bistro-inspired fare. The food is consistently good, if not the most inspired. For when you need a meal and a comforting ambiance on which you can rely.

Irish

FADO
3035 Peachtree Road NE
☎ 404-841-0066
Inexpensive-Moderate

A little bit of the "old sod" transplanted to Buckhead, Fado is a lot of fun. It really looks like an Irish pub, with pints of Guinness, fish and chips, and breakfast that can only be described as a heart attack on a plate. The name "fado" means "once upon a time" (pronounce it as "FAH-dough," with the emphasis on the first syllable). Fado is open daily for lunch and dinner.

Italian

AZIO PIZZA & PASTA
229 Peachtree Street, Peachtree Center
☎ 404-222-0808
Moderate

Azio serves contemporary Italian cuisine in a villa-style setting; menu items include brick oven-baked pizza, grilled fish and chicken, seafood, homemade pastas, and great focaccia bread. Reservations are accepted for lunch and dinner daily, 11-4 and 5-closing.

BERTOLINI'S
3500 Peachtree Road (Phipps Plaza)
☎ 404-233-2333
Moderate

A long-time Atlanta favorite, with a menu that represents a wide range of Italian cuisine. Homemade pastas, signature sauces, and fresh salads combine with consistently good service at a reasonable price.

LA GROTTA
2637 Peachtree Road NE
☎ 404-231-1368
Expensive-Deluxe

This elegant, Northern Italian eatery has been a favorite of Atlanta for more than two decades, and it deserves every bit of its popularity. Selections such as roasted quail stuffed with Italian sausage and beef tenderloin grilled with Barolo mustard are long-time favorites. La Grotta serves dinner, Mondays-Saturdays.

MAGGIANO'S LITTLE ITALY
3368 Peachtree Road
☎ 404-816-9650
Inexpensive-Moderate

Share some of the dishes at Maggiano's; the portions are huge.

In this throwback to the '50s, you'd almost expect Mario Lanza to burst into song. The portions are more than generous. Signature dishes include shrimp oreganata, rosemary chicken, and veal scallopini. you may never get past the appetizers, which include bruschetta, stuffed mushrooms and calamari fritte.

PRICCI
500 Pharr Road
☎ 404-237-2941
Expensive

Upscale informality are the bywords of this chi-chi Italian eatery. It's owned by the same group that runs the Buckhead Diner, so it is as trendy as its soul mate. A favorite on the menu is the cold water lobster tails sautéed in garlic, lemon and Pinot Grigio. Save room for a dessert of cappuccino and crème brûlée.

Seafood

ATLANTA FISH MARKET
265 Pharr Road
☎ 404-262-3165
Expensive

The place for fresh fish in Atlanta. Good selection and fast service, but not worth the wait you sometimes must endure. Easy to find, with the giant fish sculpture looming over the Pharr Road entrance.

Open for lunch Mondays-Saturdays, 11:30-2:30, and dinner daily, 5:30-11 pm.

JIM WHITE'S HALF SHELL
2349 Peachtree Road
☎ 404-237-9924
Expensive

A Buckhead staple, this restaurant has been serving up stone crab claws, Maryland crab cakes and rock lobster tails for a long time. Locals love the casual-but-dressy atmosphere. Open for dinner Mondays-Thursdays, 5-10 pm; Fridays and Saturdays, 5-11.

PERCY'S FISH HOUSE
3227 Roswell Road
☎ 404-237-3227
Moderate-Expensive

Buckhead's casual seafood restaurant. Raw bar, fried and grilled specials.

Southern

BLUE RIDGE GRILL
1261 West Paces Ferry Road
☎ 404-233-5030
Expensive

A warm tribute to the Blue Ridge mountains. Dine amidst a large stacked-stone fireplace, old timbers, painted log walls and red leather booths. Hickory grilled meats, veggies served "family-style," home-made breads and sumptuous desserts.

HORSERADISH GRILL
4320 Powers Ferry Road at Chastain Park
☎ 404-255-7277
Expensive

Here's Southern cuisine with a twist. You'll find Georgia mountain trout grilled over live hickory and North Carolina barbeque on a corn cake among the regional specials. The atmosphere is Southern comfortable. You can even dine outside if weather permits. Reservations strongly recommended.

Steaks

ANTHONY'S
3109 Piedmont Avenue
☎ 404-262-7379
Moderate-Expensive

One of the restaurants Scarlett would have on her top ten list of ways never to go hungry again. This is a romantic, restored 1797 plantation home in yuppie central Buckhead. Dine in one of 12 beautifully decorated rooms, on fare that ranges from filet mignon to fish. Open for dinner, Mondays-Saturdays.

BLUE RIDGE GRILL
1261 West Paces Ferry Road
☎ 404-233-5030
Expensive

A warm tribute to the Blue Ridge mountains. Dine amidst a large stacked-stone fireplace, old timbers, painted log walls and red leather booths. Hickory grilled meats, veggies served "family-style," homemade breads and sumptuous desserts.

BONES
3130 Piedmont Road
☎ 404-237-2663
Expensive-Deluxe

Where Atlanta's movers and shakers come to graze. Bones is a must if you are entertaining on an expense account. The clubby atmosphere, traditional steak house food, and 10,000-bottle wine gallery make it a great place to eat. The fax machines, TVs, VCRs, and private dining rooms with telephones make it the place to power dine. Bones is open daily; they serve lunch and dinner during the week and dinner only on Saturdays and Sundays.

CHOPS AND THE LOBSTER BAR
70 West Paces Ferry Road at Peachtree St.
☎ 404-262-2675
Expensive

Exceptional steaks and seafood served in a classic, yet state-of-the-art environment. A "power dining" favorite, serving lunch on weekdays and dinner Saturdays and Sundays.

HORSERADISH GRILL
4320 Powers Ferry Road at Chastain Park
☎ 404-255-7277
Expensive

Here's Southern cuisine with a twist. You'll find Georgia mountain trout grilled over live hickory and North Carolina barbeque on a corn cake among the regional specials. The atmosphere is southern comfortable. You can even dine outside if weather permits. Reservations strongly recommended.

MACARTHUR'S CHOP & CRAB HOUSE
2171 Peachtree Road
☎ 404-352-3400
Expensive

If you can't live without prime rib, this is the place.

Vegetarian

BROADWAY CAFE
2166 Briarcliff Road
☎ 404-329-0888
Inexpensive

Pastas, sautées, stirfries, homemade soups and hearty sandwiches. Fresh seafood specials are served for lunch and dinner daily.

Vinings

Brunch

CANOE
4199 Paces Ferry Road
☎ 770-432-26 630
Expensive

Spectacular views of the Chattahoochee River blend seamlessly with melt-in-your-mouth salmon and ridiculously rich hollandaise sauce over the eggs Benedict. Definitely worth the drive from downtown Atlanta, Canoe serves lunch Mondays-Fridays, dinner Mondays-Saturdays, and brunch on Sundays.

RAY'S ON THE RIVER
6700 Powers Ferry Road NW
☎ 770-955-1187
Moderate-Expensive

If you can't find something you like at this 70-item buffet, you're just too fussy. The omelets made to order are a brunch staple. Reservations are a must for Sunday brunch. Open for lunch and dinner Tuesdays through Saturdays; live jazz and freshly flown-in seafood make this a favorite with locals.

SQUID ROE COASTAL CUISINE
2940 Johnson Ferry Road
☎ 770-587-FISH
Moderate-Expensive

A little touch of Florida moved north to Cobb County, and into the back of a rather nondescript shopping center. Try the "squid of the day" or a more traditional yellowfin tuna topped with large crabs stuffed with shrimp and hollandaise.

Virginia-Highland

Asian

SURIN OF THAILAND
810 North Highland Avenue NE
☎ 404-892-7789
Expensive

Surin of Thailand is open daily for lunch and dinner, and is a neighborhood favorite with the Virginia-Highland residents. The tables are so close together you won't be able to hold a private conversation. But

Try the Pad Prik, a spicy hot dish with bell peppers and garlic with pork that is a specialty at Surin of Thailand.

don't worry, you'll be too busy concentrating on the food.

Bars & Pubs

MANUEL'S TAVERN
602 North Highland Avenue NE
☎ 404-525-3447
Inexpensive

If you're searching for a politician or journalist after hours, this is the place to look. You'll find them munching away on exceptional burgers. It can be hectic on a busy night, but the atmosphere is friendly and inviting. Manuel's is open for lunch and dinner, Mondays-Saturdays from 11 am-2 am, and Sundays from 11 am-12:30 am.

Brunch

BABETTE'S CAFE
471 North Highland Avenue NE
☎ 404-523-9121
Expensive

You'll wish this was a bed-and-breakfast. Euro-style fare is served in a charming, country French-style room. The grilled swordfish with rosemary potatoes, olives, and artichokes will have you dreaming of the Mediterranean. Babette's serves dinner from Tuesdays-Saturdays, and brunch and dinner on Sundays.

MURPHY'S
997 Virginia Avenue NE
☎ 404-872-0904
Moderate

Restaurants come and go quickly in Virginia-High-land, but Murphy's remains a fixture. A neighbor-hood favorite for its fresh, simply prepared foods, like a skillet of potatoes topped with eggs over-easy and melted cheese.

French

BABETTE'S CAFE
471 North Highland Avenue NE
☎ 404-523-9121
Expensive

Among Babette's unusual appetizers are the baby turnips and wild mushrooms in a wine and butter sauce. Babette's serves dinner from Tuesdays-Sat-urdays, and brunch and dinner on Sundays.

Lebanese

NICOLA'S
1602 La Vista Road
☎ 404-325-2524
Inexpensive

A lively and friendly neighborhood restaurant in the vicinity of Emory University, with delicious and healthy entrées. Dinner daily; lunch for parties of 12 or more with a reservation.

Pizza

EVERYBODY'S FAMOUS PIZZA
1040 N. Highland Avenue
☎ 404-873-4545
Inexpensive

This restaurant serves pizza that is thin, crispy, and delightful.

Chamblee-Tucker

Asian

PENANG MAYLAYSIAN
4897 Buford Highway NE
☎ 770-220-0308
Inexpensive-Moderate

Do not be dismayed by the tacky tropical beach décor; a fascinating array of dishes awaits you inside. Very fresh foods, particularly the prawns in a variety of sauces. Penang Maylaysian is open daily for lunch and dinner.

Little Five Points

Brunch

THE FLYING BISCUIT CAFE
1655McLendon Avenue NE
☎ 404-687-8888
Inexpensive-Moderate

Fist-sized biscuits, black bean cakes, organic oat-meal pancakes and turkey meat loaf are staples at this eatery. Breakfast, lunch and dinner are served Tuesdays-Sundays, and there's almost always a massive line for brunch on Saturdays and Sundays; expect a wait of at least an hour.

French

CAFE BOHEME
453 Moreland Avenue NE
☎ 404-522-4373
Moderate

French bistro fare as classic as it comes. White paper covers on the tables and smoky jazz on the stereo complete the ambiance.

Best Places to Eat

Beyond Atlanta

Atlantans once viewed I-285 as a great concrete moat, dividing the city from the suburbia. Once, there were clear distinctions between Atlanta and surrounding municipalities such as Marietta, Kennesaw, Roswell and Smyrna. But now you can travel outside the Perimeter into neighboring counties with barely a breach in the strip malls and subdivisions. Without the occasional sign alerting you to the changing city limits, many drivers would be hard pressed to define where Atlanta stops.

Visitors looking for adventures beyond the city should consider a day-trip to one or several of these diverse communities; they are rich in history, natural beauty and serious shopping opportunities.

Just Outside the Perimeter

Orientation

North

Much of central Atlanta is within **Fulton County**; outside the Perimeter, the towns of northern Fulton and **DeKalb** Counties, including Sandy Springs, Roswell, Alpharetta and Dunwoody, have a close relationship with the city. These towns are off GA 400/

US 19, and are within approximately 25 miles of Atlanta.

Alpharetta

Once a small farmland community in the foothills of
the Appalachian Mountains, this town has blossomed into one of the city's up-and-coming suburbs;
its planned communities are filled with high-profile
executives and local celebrities.

The Alpharetta Welcome Center is located at 20
North Main Street, ☎ 678-297-0102, www.alpha-
rettacvb.com.

Roswell

Just 20 miles north of Atlanta, in the foothills of the
Georgia Mountains on GA 400, this charming community began in the 1830s as a mill town along the
banks of Vickery Creek where it flows into the Chattahoochee River. As the mills and the community
flourished, antebellum mansions rose along the west
bank of the creek. The most famous of these is
Bulloch Hall, built in 1839. This was the home of
Theodore Roosevelt's mother, Mittie Bulloch.

Much of the original mill village of Historic Roswell
has been restored, with period storefronts containing specialty shops and restaurants dotting the historic district. Just perfect for afternoon strolling.

Northeast

Originally part of Georgia's Indian Territory, **Gwinnett County** was created by the State Legislature
in 1818. The county was named for Button Gwinnett, the third signer of the Declaration of Independence and a former state governor.

Once largely rural, with small towns, country stores, and family farms, Gwinnett County is now home to more than 200 international companies and 450 high-tech firms, as well as the Mall of Georgia, in Buford. The area has blossomed to include some of the most exclusive neighborhoods in the Atlanta metropolitan area. The towns of Braselton, Buford, Duluth, Lawrenceville, Lilburn and Norcross are all located off I-85 in Gwinnett County.

You can contact the Gwinnett County Convention & Visitors Bureau, www.gcvb.org, ☎ 888-494-6638.

East

The city of Atlanta spills over almost imperceptibly from Fulton into **DeKalb County**; neighborhoods such as Druid Hills and Little Five Points are actually in DeKalb County.

But the county deserves recognition as a distinct area. **Decatur**, the county seat, grew up around its courthouse, and in recent years this area has undergone a renaissance; small storefronts have been preserved, and new dining and entertainment establishments have sprung up. DeKalb County is also home to **Agnes Scott College**, **Emory University**, and **Stone Mountain**.

The DeKalb County Convention & Visitors Bureau can be reached at www.atlantasdekalb.org, ☎ 800-999-6055 ext 117.

Southeast

Clayton County, just 18 miles south of Atlanta off I-75, is the home of Jonesboro, one of the inspirations for Margaret Mitchell's classic novel, *Gone*

With The Wind. This area transports visitors back almost 150 years to the plantation lifestyle era. The **Road To Tara Museum**, housed in the old train depot, is filled with all sorts of Rhett and Scarlett memorabilia, such as film props, reproductions of costumes, and film photography.

The area is not so firmly entrenched in history that it hasn't left room for a lively present. You'll discover the **Atlanta Motor Speedway** of NASCAR fame, in the Henry County town of Hampton; the **Atlanta State Farmers Market**; and **Spivey Hall**, the concert hall at Clayton State College in Morrow, GA, that attracts the finest international musicians and vocalists.

For more information, call the Clayton County Convention & Visitors Bureau, ☎ 770-478-4800.

South

This is the area most visitors see first, as south **Fulton County** is the home of Hartsfield Atlanta International Airport, one of the busiest in North America. South Fulton County retains much of Atlanta's railroad presence, with its many sprawling rail lines. It's a residential community as well, with older towns such as College Park, as well as newer planned developments. South Fulton County is also home to the South's only velodrome, located in East Point.

West

To the west of Atlanta along I-20 is southern **Cobb County**, the home of Six Flags theme park (page 204). The town of **Douglasville** has a downtown area listed on the National Register of Historic Places, and is the home of Arbor Place Mall (see *Shopping*, page 216).

Northwest

Cobb County came into being in 1832 when the state redistributed land once belonging to the Cherokee Nation. It is named for Thomas Welch Cobb, an early settler in the region. Much of the county was devastated during the battle of Kennesaw Mountain (see page 91).

Today, the towns of Cobb County, although considered bedroom communities for Atlanta, have histories and personalities of their own.

For information, call the Cobb County Convention & Visitors Bureau, ☎ 678-909-COBB (2622) or 800-451-3480, www.cobbcvb.com.

Marietta

The charming community of Marietta, a short 15 miles northwest of Atlanta off I-75, offers a glimpse of the South's vivid and dramatic past. The picturesque town square is perfect for shopping and strolling, and the **Marietta/Cobb Museum of Art** showcases a permanent collection of works by Southern artists.

Walking tours escort visitors past immaculately maintained 19th-century mansions that ooze with the charm of *Gone With The Wind*.

Marietta has five National Register Historic Districts containing more than 150 antebellum and Victorian homes. The **Kennesaw House**, where Major General William Tecumseh Sherman slept before marching into Atlanta, is now home to the **Marietta Museum of History**, located on the second floor.

Marietta is also home to the **big chicken**, a well-known and well-loved area landmark. Don't be surprised to hear many Atlantans give directions that include, "go past the big chicken."

Vinings

If antiques call to you with a siren song, Vinings is the place to go. Antique shops and high-rise businesses mix dramatically within this pre-Civil War area, which was founded as a getaway for early Atlantans. Vinings boasts several preserved sites such as the **Pace House** and the **Old Vinings Inn**.

Located on the Cobb County side of I-285, Vinings' close proximity to Buckhead, Downtown, Cumberland Mall, the interstates, and the Chattahoochee River, combine to make this a good hotel location beyond the Perimeter.

Attractions

There's no shortage of amusements and attractions just beyond the perimeter road surrounding Atlanta. You could spend an entire week without ever setting foot into downtown Atlanta, and never run out of things to do.

North

CHATTAHOOCHEE NATURE CENTER
9135 Willeo Road
Roswell
☎ 770-992-2055

Spread over 127 acres in north Fulton County, the Chattahoochee Nature Center has both indoor and outdoor exhibits of native wildlife, trails through the forest, and a boardwalk along the Chattahoochee River.

To reach the Nature Center from Atlanta, take GA 400 north to Exit 6 (Northridge); bear right and go back over the freeway, then take an immediate right at Dunwoody Place. Proceed 1.2 miles to Roswell Road, then turn right and cross the river. Take the first left at Azalea Drive, and another left at Willeo Road. The Nature Center is on the right.

Northeast

CHATEAU ELAN RESORT AND WINERY
100 Tour de France
Braselton
☎ 678-425-0900 or 800-233-WINE (9463), www.chateauelan.com

A 16th-century-style château is the focal point of this 3,100-acre complex containing vineyards, a winery, three championship golf courses, a European-style health spa, and tennis center.

Château Elan is about 40 minutes northeast of Atlanta in Gwinnett County. Take I-85 to Exit 126; turn left onto Highway 211 and cross over the interstate. The Winery, Inn, and Spa are the first gate on

The Château Elan Winery has received more than 200 medals of excellence since it opened in 1984. The Château produces 15 varieties of wine. Winery tours are available.

Beyond Atlanta

the left; the par 3 golf course is the second gate, and the Golf Clubhouse (the Château and the Woodlands), and Real Estate are the third gate. For Spa information, see page 119.

LAKE LANIER ISLANDS RESORT
6950 Holiday Road
Lake Lanier Islands
☎ 770-932-7200

Lake Lanier Islands is a full-service resort on one of the most popular lakes in the state. Over 1,200 acres of recreational facilities surrounded by 38,000 acres of water offers a multitude of activities, including the Lake Lanier Islands Beach and Water Park, and stables.

Lake Lanier is approximately 35 miles north of Atlanta. Take I-85 north to I-985 (Gainesville exit). From I-985 take Exit 8-Friendship Road; turn left and continue for five miles. The road ends at Lake Lanier Islands Resort.

YELLOW RIVER WILDLIFE GAME RANCH
4525 Highway 78
Lilburn
Admission: $6 for adults, $5 for children
Hours: Daily, 9:30 am to dusk
☎ 770-972-6643

More than 600 native Georgia animals, some rarely seen elsewhere in the state, roam 24 wooded acres of this wildlife reserve; there is also a petting zoo.

Lilburn is approximately 20 miles northeast of Atlanta. Take I-285 to exit 39B, onto Highway 78 east. after 10 miles, cross the Yellow River Bridge. The ranch is the first driveway on the left after the bridge.

East

STONE MOUNTAIN PARK
US Highway 78
Stone Mountain
Admission: $16 for adults, $13 ages three to 11
Parking: $6 per vehicle
Hours: Park, 6 am-midnight; attraction hours vary
☎ 770-498-5690, www.stonemountainpark.com
MARTA: #120 Stone Mountain bus from Avondale
Station, transfer to #19 bus

You'll find Stone Mountain just 16 miles east of Atlanta, in DeKalb county. Originally known as New Gibraltar, the town was burned in Sherman's March to the Sea. The town was rebuilt after the war and is now called The Village of Stone Mountain. Stone Mountain itself is a marvel of man and nature. The world's largest exposed granite outcropping is the canvas for the world's largest bas-relief sculpture, a carving of Confederate President Jefferson Davis and generals Stonewall Jackson and Robert E. Lee. Within the park you'll find a skylift, a paddlewheel riverboat, an antebellum plantation, wildlife preserve and petting zoo, plus beaches and water slides, an antique auto museum, miniature golf, and tennis. Stone Mountain Park is one of the most popular attractions in the United States, with four million visitors annually.

South

ATLANTA BEACH AT CLAYTON COUNTY INTERNATIONAL PARK
2300 Hwy. 138
Jonesboro
☎ 770-477-3766

Site of the 1996 Olympics beach volleyball competition, this facility offers swimming, beach volleyball, golf, paddleboats and fishing.

West

SIX FLAGS OVER GEORGIA
7561 Six Flags Road at I-20 West
Mableton
☎ 770-948-9290
www. sixflags.com

Six Flags Over Georgia presents family-friendly fun for all ages. Highlights include heart-pounding rides, live Broadway-style shows, and other thrilling attractions.

The park is located in southern Cobb County, about 10 miles from Douglasville. From central Atlanta, take I-20/GA 402 west across the river. Turn left at Six Flags Parkway and follow the signs for the park entrance.

Check the web site or call the park for information on admission prices.

Northwest

AMERICAN ADVENTURES AMUSEMENT PARK
250 Cobb Parkway
Marietta
Admission is $15 for all attractions; admission to Foam Factory only is $8 for kids; $3 for parents and $5 for toddlers.
☎ 770-424-9283

Georgia's only amusement park designed especially for families with children features rides for all ages. The Foam Factory Funhouse is for kids up to age 15. There's also mini-golf and go-cart racing.

The park is open seasonally only, from May to Labor Day. From Atlanta, take I-75 north to Exit 265 and follow the signs.

WHITE WATER THEME PARK
250 North Marietta Parkway
Marietta
Admission: $23 for adults, $15 for children three to four feet tall, plus tax.
Hours: Open weekends only in May, daily from Memorial Day to Labor Day.
☎ 770-424-9283

This water theme park spread over almost 40 acres is one of the largest water parks in the country, and it includes attractions that are both thrilling and relaxing.

Historic & Cultural Activities

North

BULLOCH HALL
180 Bulloch Avenue
Roswell
☎ 770-992-1731

Built in 1840, this was the childhood home of Mittie Bulloch, the bride of Theodore Roosevelt, Sr. and the mother of President Theodore Roosevelt, the 26th President of the United States.

Bulloch Hall is in Historic Roswell, off GA 9 (Roswell Road/Atlanta Street).

DUNWOODY STAGE DOOR PLAYERS
5339 Chamblee Road
Dunwoody
☎ 770-396-8092

This non-profit, community-based theater offers quality productions of classic and contemporary comedies, dramas and musicals. The theater is located in Dunwoody. Call for performance schedules and ticket information.

SMITH PLANTATION HOME
935 Alpharetta Street
Roswell
Admission: $5 for adults, $3 for children
Hours: Tours are conducted Mondays-Fridays, 11 am
and 2 pm; Saturdays at 11 am, noon, and 1 pm.
☎ 770-641-3978

The antebellum home was constructed in 1845 and
has working outbuildings, including a cook house,
carriage house, spring house, barn and slave cabin.

Northeast

GWINNETT FINE ARTS CENTER
6400 Sugarloaf Parkway
Duluth
Admission: $3
☎ 770-623-6002

The Gwinnett Fine Arts Center is a non-profit organization that features mixed media, photography,
sculpture and other fine arts.

SOUTHEASTERN RAILWAY MUSEUM
3996 Buford Highway
Duluth
☎ 770-476-2013, www.srmduluth.org

Over 70 pieces of rolling stock, including vintage
steam locomotives, historic wooden cars, and Pull-
mans (including the 1911 car "Superb" used by President Harding during his Presidency), can be seen
up-close at this 12-acre site.

The Railway Museum is open Saturdays from 9-5,
and the third Sunday of each month from noon to
5 pm.

Beyond Atlanta

South

SPIVEY HALL
Clayton State College
5900 N. Lee Street
Morrow
☎ 770-961-3683

Intimate and elegant, Spivey Hall is known as the "Carnegie Hall of the South," and presents the highest level of musical performance from classical to jazz.

Northwest

MARIETTA/COBB MUSEUM OF ART
30 Atlanta Street
Marietta
☎ 770-528-1444

The only museum in the Atlanta area to focus on American Art, this museum provides visitors with exposure to visual arts through exhibitions and services.

THEATRE IN THE SQUARE
11 Whitlock Avenue
Marietta
☎ 770-422-8369

The professional company that makes its home in a former cotton warehouse attracts the second-largest audience of any metro-Atlanta theater. Recent productions have included *Hedda Gabler*, *Moon Over Buffalo* and *Smoke On The Mountain*. Call for current production schedule and ticket information.

Sports

Golf and tennis are the sports that dominate beyond the Perimeter, with some small attention given to hiking and water sports on Lake Lanier.

North

Hiking

AMICALOLA FALLS STATE PARK
240 Amicalola Falls State Park Road
Dawsonville
☎ 706-265-4703

This park is named for Georgia's highest waterfall, which drops 729 feet in seven cascades. The 900-acre park sits at an elevation of 3,000 feet, approximately 100 miles northwest of Atlanta (about a two-hour drive). It is here that you can take the approach path to the beginning of the Appalachian Trail. There is a choice of two trails; the eight-mile trek is an easy to moderate one, and at the end of the five-mile hike there's a lodge that serves family-style meals.

Tennis

BLACKBURN TENNIS CENTER
3501 Ashford Dunwoody Road
Dunwoody
☎ 770-451-1061

The 18 all-outdoor hard surface courts are lighted for evening play. Reservations are required at least two days in advance. The cost is $2 per hour. Clubhouse with pro shop, showers, lockers and snack bar.

Northeast

Boating & Water Sports

LAKE LANIER ISLANDS
6950 Holiday Road
Buford
☎ 770-932-7255

Ski boats, paddleboats, sailboats, pontoon boats and houseboats are available for rent at Lake Lanier Islands. The area also has a one-mile-long white sand beach, 10 water slides, a wave pool, and miniature golf.

Golf

CHATEAU ELAN
6060 Golf Club Drive
Braselton
☎ 678-42506050
www.chateauelan.com

For some serious golf, tee off at Château Elan, home of the Legends Course designed by Denis Griffiths, Gene Sarazen, Sam Snead and Kathy Whitworth. The 18-hole, par 72 private course has a yardage of 6,781. The golf club also has a driving range, practice greens and cart rentals.

Tennis

HUDLOW CENTER
2501 Old Rockridge Road
Norcross
☎ 770-417-2210

Sixteen all-outdoor hard surface courts are lighted for evening play. Reservations are required at least one day in advance; fees are $2.00 for singles, $2.50 for doubles. There's a soft drink machine, but no clubhouse or snack bar.

East

Golf

STONE MOUNTAIN GOLF COURSE
US Highway 78
Village of Stone Mountain
☎ 770-498-5690
www.stonemountainpark.com

Stone Mountain Park's 36-hole championship golf course has been named one of the top 75 public golf courses in the United States by *Golf Digest* for more than 20 years. Located 16 miles east of downtown Atlanta, the course is open daily, and features a driving range, putting green and restaurant. The clubhouse hosts a pro shop, locker rooms, and bag drop-off.

Hiking

STONE MOUNTAIN PARK
US Highway 78
Village of Stone Mountain
Admission: adults, $16; ages three-11, $13
Hours: Attraction hours vary; park is open year round, 6 am-midnight
☎ 770-498-5690
www.stonemountainpark.com

This multifaceted park, located 16 miles east of downtown Atlanta, features the world's largest exposed granite outcrop. You can hike one of two trails around the base of the outcropping, or take another that leads to the top of the mountain, at an elevation of 1,600 feet. All trails are easy to moderate. Admission to the park is all that's required.

South

Golf

LAKE SIDE GOLF CLUB
3600 Old Fairburn Road
East Point
☎ 404-344-3629

Once a private club, it's now open to the public. A recent $1 million renovation included everything from fairways to the clubhouse. You'll find a dogleg on nearly every hole that will keep you challenged.

Lake Side is located south of Atlanta, near Hartsfield Atlanta International Airport.

SOUTHERNESS GOLF CLUB
4871 Flat Bridge Road
Stockbridge
☎ 770-808-6000

Southerness has been called by *Gene's Golf Guide* "the classiest semi-private golf course in the city." This 18-hole championship course is situated in a riverside setting. Features such as curbside-to-hole valet service, first-class rental equipment, putting green and driving range round out the amenities. Stockbridge is off I-75, just south of Atlanta.

Tennis

SOUTH FULTON TENNIS CENTER
5645 Mason Road
College Park
☎ 770-306-3059

Four outdoor clay courts and 20 hard surface outdoor courts, all lighted for evening play. Two-story clubhouse with large pro shop, showers and lockers, vending machines. Reservations can be made up to three days in advance. Fees are $2 per person, per hour. For more information about tennis facilities, call the Atlanta Lawn Tennis Association at ☎ 770-399-5788.

Shopping

If you've come to shop till you drop, then the area beyond the Perimeter will be shopping nirvana for you. Atlanta has long been the mecca for shopping in the Southeast, but with the addition of several megamalls in the surrounding areas, its position is in danger of being usurped. Beyond the Perimeter, shopping is done on a grand scale; no cute little shops

Beyond Atlanta

hugging a prime position on Main Street. Here they are gathered together in major installations. Lace up your Reeboks and prepare for serious shopping.

North

NORTH GEORGIA PREMIUM OUTLETS
Dawson Forest Road
Dawsonville
☎ 706-216-3609

One of the better outlets within an hour's drive of Atlanta. All the usual suspects – Ralph Lauren, Polo, Brooks Brothers, Crate & Barrel, The Gap, Off 5th and Donna Karan Company Store.

Dawsonville is in Dawson County; take I-85 to GA 400 and continue north for about 45 miles. The mall is on the right at the intersection of Dawson Forest Road.

NORTH POINT MALL
Alpharetta
☎ 770-740-8636

A big, bustling, sprawling airy mall that is absolutely perfect for the boomtown suburbia of Alpharetta. Inside you'll find Dillard's, Rich's and Lord & Taylor.

From I-85 take GA 400 north; take Exit 9 to Haynes Bridge Road, then turn right on Haynes Bridge and go about ¼ mile. The mall entrance is on the right.

PERIMETER MALL
4400 Ashford Dunwoody Road
Dunwoody
☎ 770-394-4270

The Southeast's first Nordstrom opened shop at this mall, and joined the company of JCPenney, Rich's, Macy's, and 185 other fine stores. Across the street, you'll find Home Depot's Expo and Old Navy. Something for everyone.

This mall is just north of the Perimeter. From I-85 take I-285 West, or from GA 400 take I-285 East. Take Exit 21 and make a right off the ramp onto Ashford Dunwoody Road; the mall is on the left.

Northeast

GWINNETT PLACE
Pleasant Hill Road
Duluth
☎ 770-476-5160

Good, solid, traditional mall shopping, anchored by Macy's, Sears, Rich's, and Parisian. The traffic is mind-boggling in this area. Be brave, and hope for a parking space.

Take I-85 north to Exit 104, Pleasant Hill Road. Go west on Pleasant Hill Road; the mall will be on the right.

MALL OF GEORGIA
3333 Buford Drive
Buford
☎ 678-482-8788

They don't come any bigger than this! This shopping monster has been dropped into what once was a forest alongside an interstate. It has more upscale shops than Gwinnett Place, making it worth the extra 10-minute drive north. You'll find Nordstrom and Lord & Taylor anchoring this extravaganza.

Take I-85 to Exit 115 (GA 20W). Turn left and continue for about ¼ mile to the mall.

West

ARBOR PLACE MALL
Chapel Hill Road
Douglasville
☎ 770-947-4245

One of the newest in the area, this one features Dillard's, Old Navy, Borders Books and Music and an 18-screen movie theater. Douglasville is about 10 miles west of Six Flags Theme Park.

Take I-20 west to Exit 36 which is Chapel Hill Road. Go south to the second light at Douglas Drive and turn right. The mall is one block down Douglas Drive on the left.

CUMBERLAND MALL
1000 Cumberland Mall
Atlanta
☎ 770-435-2206

An eclectic array of stores awaits you inside the Cumberland Mall. You'll find everything from Macy's and JC Penney to Ann Taylor, bebe, and The Disney Store. Special services include Spa Sydell, 16 eateries, and a post office.

Cumberland Mall is just inside the Perimeter in the Vinings area, off Cobb Parkway near the I-75/I-285 Interchange.

After Dark

Just because you're beyond the Perimeter doesn't mean you'll have to sacrifice your night life. As the area outside of Atlanta has grown, the nightlife has grown with it. Although not as prevalent as they are Downtown, the offerings are intriguing.

Northeast

FLYING MACHINE
510 Briscoe Boulevard
Lawrenceville
☎ 770-962-2262

This one is a bit of a mix. The aeronautically themed restaurant with a runway's-edge view of the Gwinnett County Airport features country music performers.

Northwest

THE BLUE PIG
9770 S. Main Street
Woodstock
☎ 770-517-2583

A casual barbecue restaurant and bar, with televised sporting events and live music on the weekend. The usual musical fare is Texas shuffle and jump blues.

Woodstock is in Cherokee County, north of Marietta and just south of Lake Allatoona. To get there, take I-75 north to I-575. Go north on I-575, then turn left onto Highway 92 and right onto Canton Road (Main Street) in Woodstock.

Beyond Atlanta

DARWIN'S
1598 Roswell Road
Marietta
☎ 770-578-6872

A Marietta watering hole catering to the educated
blues enthusiast, with local and regional acts.

HOUCK'S
305 Village Parkway
Marietta
☎ 770-859-0041

This bustling Marietta nightspot has a large outdoor
deck, and a music room inside featuring local party
bands. Houck's has a large local following that rev-
els in the requests and singalongs. You'll hear everything from *Rocky Top* to the Rolling Stones.

Best Places To Stay

ACCOMMODATIONS PRICE SCALE	
Inexpensive	$50-$100
Moderate	$100-$150
Expensive	$150-$200
Deluxe	more than $200

North

CROWNE PLAZA RAVINIA
4355 Ashford-Dunwoody Road
Dunwoody, GA 30346
☎ 770-395-7700 or 800-554-0055
Deluxe

A pretty hotel with a hint of luxury. The 459 rooms are spacious, and decorated in neutral color schemes with light pine furniture. On-site are four restaurants, indoor and outdoor pools, a health club, convention center and business services.

W ATLANTA HOTEL @ perimeter center
111 Perimeter Center West
Atlanta, GA 30346
☎ 770-396-6800 or 877-946-8357
www.whotels.com
Deluxe

The "W" hotels (for warm, witty and welcoming) are Starwood's new signature collection of hotels for the trendy set. Chic and metropolitan in style, the rooms provide laptop hookups, internet access, data ports and modems. Tired of all that work? Fall asleep in beds with 250-thread-count linens and goosedown comforters. Even the lobby is chi-chi, with games of chess, other board games, and candles, all designed to create a "living room" feel. The hotel is approximately 45 minutes north of the airport.

Beyond Atlanta

Northeast

CHATEAU ELAN
100 Tour de France
Braselton, GA 30517
☎ 678-425-0900 or 800-233-WINE (9436)
www.chateauelan.com
Deluxe

Château Elan offers many special golf, tennis and spa packages.

This French-inspired château complex just 45 minutes to an hour northeast of Atlanta will transport you to another world. Each of the resort's deluxe rooms include an oversize bath with separate garden tub and shower, three dual-line telephones, a personal safe, and minibar.

The Château Elan resort includes a 25,000-square-foot conference center, 170-acre golf course, a Stan Smith-designed seven-court tennis center, an equestrian show center, horseback and nature trails, a full service spa, and more than 200 acres of vineyards producing a variety of wines.

East

EVERGREEN CONFERENCE CENTER & RESORT
4021 Lakeview Dr.
Village of Stone Mountain, GA 30083
☎ 770-879-9900
www.evergreenresort.com
Expensive

Managed by Marriott, the Evergreen Conference Center and Resort is ranked as one of the top meeting facilities in the United States. The resort features a restaurant, sports bar, health club and tennis.

HOLIDAY INN SELECT
4386 Chamblee Dunwoody Road
Chamblee, GA 30341
☎ 770-457-9628, 800-535-0707
Moderate-Expensive

This upscale Holiday Inn, one mile east of Perimeter Mall and eight miles from Buckhead, has 250 rooms with in-room work desks, voice mail, cable TVs, data ports and coffee makers. Ideal for the business traveler. On-site amenities include an outdoor swimming pool, the Bristol Bar and Grille, a fitness room and laundry.

STONE MOUNTAIN INN
78 Stone Mountain Parkway
Village of Stone Mountain, GA 30086
☎ 770-469-3311
Moderate

A classic Southern inn located near the entrance to the park, the 92-room hotel features banquet and meeting facilities and a southern-style restaurant.

STONE MOUNTAIN FAMILY CAMPGROUND
☎ 770-498-5710 or 800-385-9807
www.stonemountainpark.com/lodging/campground
Inexpensive

The 441-site campground features primitive tent sites, partial hook-up and full hook-up sites. The campground has lake sites, a supply store, laundry facilities, volleyball court and playground.

Beyond Atlanta

South

HOLIDAY INN SOUTH
6288 Old Dixie Highway
Jonesboro, GA 30236
☎ 770-968-4300, 800-535-0707
Moderate

Just seven miles from Hartsfield Atlanta International Airport and 13 miles from downtown Atlanta, this is an excellent choice for the budget traveler. Facilities at this 180-room hotel include a seasonal outdoor pool, an exercise facility, complimentary morning coffee, cable TV, and in-room coffee makers.

Best Places To Eat

DINING PRICE SCALE
Price scale reflects the cost of an average entrée.
Inexpensive . . . . $5-$10
Moderate . . . . $10-$25
Expensive. . . . . $25-$50
Deluxe . . . . More than $50

North

ALTOBELI'S FINE ITALIAN CUISINE
3000 Old Alabama Road (Haynes Bridge Road)
Alpharetta
☎ 770-664-8055
Moderate

Traditional Italian food in a cozy atmosphere of wood paneled rooms. The food and service are sometimes erratic, but when they connect, it's *bellissima*. Altobeli's is open for dinner daily from 5 pm; reservations are recommended.

EL ZORITO
880 Atlanta Street
Roswell
☎ 770-998-6553
Inexpensive

The old Tex-Mex standbys will not disappoint you. For a little more adventure, try the *puerco enguajillo*, pork strips cooked in a red chili sauce. *Ay Caramba*!

LA GROTTA
4355 Ashford Dunwoody Road
Crowne Plaza Ravinia
Dunwoody
☎ 770-395-9925, www.la-grotta.com
Expensive

La Grotta specializes in Northern Italian cuisine. House specialties include homemade pasta so light it practically floats off your plate. La Grotta has earned AAA's prestigious Four Diamond Award, and a Reader's Choice Award from *Gourmet* magazine.

Northeast

CRIPPLE CREEK
3525 Mall Blvd.
Duluth
☎ 770-497-4228
Moderate

Burgers, pizza and steaks served in an L. L. Bean atmosphere. Not exactly a mountain lodge, but pretty close.

MAYLAYAN VILLAGE
3312 Peachtree Industrial Blvd.
Duluth
☎ 678-473-9889
Moderate

An exotic dining experience that takes Southeast Asian flavors and serves them up in a kitschy, quasi-tropical décor. Think Thai meets Polynesian.

MINA'S PLACE
6889 Peachtree Industrial Blvd.
Norcross
☎ 770-242-0305
Inexpensive

Memorable West African cuisine, including jerk chicken. The more adventurous should try dishes such as joloff rice, fish in palm oil, and fufu. The menu is fascinating; be brave.

East

FLOATAWAY CAFE
1123 Zonolite Road
Decatur, GA (Emory University area)
☎ 404-892-1414
Tuesdays-Saturdays, 5-10 pm (dinner only)
Expensive

This is a Mediterranean café with overtones of California Cuisine. Try the chanterelle pizza. And don't be misled by the casual ambiance into thinking that this will be an inexpensive meal; with a bottle of wine and three courses, it may be a pricey evening.

SUSHI AVENUE
308 Ponce de Leon Avenue
Decatur, GA
☎ 404-378-8448
Open daily for dinner; lunch is served Mondays-Fridays
Moderate

Sushi Avenue is a small, pretty, and unassuming little restaurant that consistently serves up fresh sushi. The presentation will make you think you've wandered into a sushi bar in Tokyo by mistake. If you don't like sushi, try the buckwheat noodles with tempura, or donburi rice bowls with breaded pork cutlets.

Beyond Atlanta

THUMBS UP DINER
573 Edgewood Avenue, Old Fourth Ward
Decatur, GA
☎ 404-223-0690
Open 7 am-3 pm, breakfast and lunch only
Inexpensive

If you like stone-ground grits, buckwheat pancakes, and your orange juice fresh and pulpy, this is one of the best places in town for breakfast or brunch. It's a modest establishment in a "transitional" neighborhood, so expect good food but not a great location.

South

HISTORIC GREEN MANOR
6400 Westbrook Street
Union City
☎ 770-964-4343
Inexpensive-Moderate

Miss Emma's made-from-scratch desserts keep regulars coming back. The Green family calls their big, buffet-style lunch and brunch, "elegant Southern." Luscious roast meats, fried chicken, and fresh vegetables are highlights of the menu.

TRUETT'S GRILL
2042 Mount Zion Road
Morrow
☎ 770-210-0500
Inexpensive

A '50s-style diner named in honor of Chick-fil-A® founder S. Truett Cathy is a fitting tribute. The prices can't be beat. And the kids will get a kick out of the restored cars in the parking lot.

Northwest

BACKYARD BURGERS
1323 Johnson Ferry Road
Marietta
☎ 770-509-0444
Inexpensive

This East Cobb County drive-through restaurant is as close to a rolling barbecue as you can find. Toppings such as coleslaw and grilled pineapple mean you really can have it your way.

FOWL PLAY CAFE
3161 North Cobb Pkwy
Kennesaw
☎ 770-966-9686
Inexpensive

Buffalo-style in five degrees of heat, chicken's the thing here, especially those wings slathered with honey mustard, teriyaki and other flavors.

HAMILTON'S
500 Powder Springs Road
Marietta Conference Center
Marietta
☎ 770-427-2500
Moderate-Expensive

Classical dining on the site of the old Georgia Military Institute has tables both inside and outside. Open daily for breakfast, lunch and dinner. Elegant, yet affordable and familiar.

HASIGUCHI JAPANESE RESTAURANT
300 Windy Hill Road
Marietta
☎ 770-955-2337
Moderate-Expensive

Japanese cuisine for those wanting more than just tempura and soba noodles. Upscale and soothing with superior service.

INDIA'S OVEN
1477 Roswell Road
Marietta
☎ 770-971-1166
Inexpensive-Moderate

The chef's sense of spicing is evident in the chutneys, tandooris and other traditional fare. This is an unassuming little spot that's worth exploring.

Regional Tours

Atlantans love to drive, so it won't come as a surprise that they think nothing of leaping into the ol' family SUV and heading out with the speed of a NASCAR driver in second place on the last lap. But you can't blame them for their road trip fever, as there is so much to see within a short drive.

Nature lovers can get their fill at Callaway Gardens, home to a butterfly conservatory, or at the Tennessee Aquarium in Chattanooga, where you can observe scuba divers feeding giant catfish and sharks.

Can't get to Germany for the Oktoberfest? You can fill up on oom-pah-pah in Helen, Georgia's own alpine village.

And if history is your heart's desire, visit the Etowah Indian Mounds, the well-preserved site of mounds built from AD 1000-1500. Civil War buffs will yearn to walk the battlefield of Chickamauga, where you can almost hear the sound of cannon fire.

Need the sound of the ocean in your ear or simply yearn for a walk on the beach? Try the Golden Isles or Cumberland Island.

So fill up the tank of that rental car and join the locals in the ritual of the weekend road trip!

North

AMICALOLA FALLS STATE PARK & LODGE
240 Amicalola Falls State Park Road (Info)
418 Amicalola Falls Lodge Road (Lodge)
Dawsonville, GA 30534
Hours: Park, 7 am to 10 pm; office, 8-5
☎ 800-573-9656 or 706-265-8888 (reservations); 706-265-4703 (park); www.ganet.org/dnr/parks or http://ngeorgia.com/parks/amicalola

Georgia's most-visited state park is home to a 729-foot crystalline cascade that attracts nearly two million shutterbugs and hikers a year. Hike the trails around the base or to the top fall, depending on your level of fitness. Keep an eye open for pileated woodpeckers, white-tailed deer and black bears.

Lodge accommodations include rooms and suites; some are handicapped accessible. There are also 20 cabins with one, two, or three bedrooms, and 20 campsites with water and electricity.

From Atlanta, take GA 400 north to GA 53; turn left toward Dawsonville. Turn right onto Elliott Family Parkway (Hwy 183). Continue on 183 until it ends, then turn right on GA 52. Entrance to the park is on the left, a mile past Burt's Pumpkin Farm.

CHICKAMAUGA BATTLEFIELD
US Highway 27
Fort Oglethorpe
☎ 706-866-6627

More than 600 monuments and markers depict battle lines and commemorate casualties at this Civil War historical site in the northwest corner of Georgia, only 92 miles from downtown Atlanta, on the outskirts of Chattanooga, TN. The visitor center houses the Fuller Gun Collection, which features 355 weapons dating from the Revolutionary War through World War II.

Chickamauga is just south of the Tennessee border, outside Chattanooga. Take I-75 north, then head west on Route 2 to Oglethorpe. From there, take GA 27 to Chickamauga.

HELEN, GA
Georgia's Alpine Village
☎ 800-858-8027, www.helenga.org (Welcome Center)

This Bavarian-themed village, 85 miles (about 1½ hours) from downtown Atlanta, is cute and kitschy, and only just a little over the top. People love to stroll the streets of specialty shops that sell handmade goods and holiday decorations. It's packed during Oktoberfest, but at other times you won't have to wait too long to drink German-style beer in the beer gardens and eateries.

From I-85, go north to the Gainesville/I-985 exit. Go 42 miles, continuing north on Highway 365, to Highway 384. Turn left onto 384 and go 16 miles to Highway 75. Turn right and go three miles into Helen.

TENNESSEE AQUARIUM
1 Broad Street
Chattanooga, TN
☎ 800-262-0695
www.tnaqua.org

This popular Chattanooga attraction, just 115 miles (approximately two hours) from downtown Atlanta on I-75, is the largest freshwater aquarium in the world, holding more than 9,000 fish, birds, mammals, reptiles and amphibians. After you tour the 12-story complex, you can rest your feet in the IMAX 3D theater next door. Kids will love this one.

South

CALLAWAY GARDENS
205 N. Cherry Street
Pine Mountain, GA
Admission: $10 adults, $5 children over five
☎ 800-225-5292, www.callawaygardens.org

Only 70 miles from downtown Atlanta, Callaway Gardens is another world. The 2,500-acre botanical park north of Columbus features more than 700 varieties of azaleas – many displayed in the 40-acre Azalea Bowl – as well as hundreds of other types of plants and a butterfly center where thousands of the insects fly free. At Christmas time, Callaway Gardens holds a holiday extravaganza (see page 25).

From Atlanta, take I-85 south; when the highway splits, continue south on I-185 to the exit for US Hwy 27. Go left on Hwy 27 for approximately 10 miles to Callaway Gardens.

Beyond Atlanta

CUMBERLAND ISLAND
NATIONAL SEASHORE
☎ 912-882-4336

The largest of Georgia's barrier reef islands, Cumberland Island is a subtropical paradise and protected national seashore. Most of its attractions are natural ones – long, wide beaches, shell-gravel paths through forests of moss-draped live oaks, and wild horses left over from the days of the Spanish occupation. A number of structures built by the family of Thomas Carnegie (brother of Andrew) remain, including the ruins of a mansion at Dungeness, a vacant house called Plum Orchard, and Greyfield, the exclusive lodge where John F. Kennedy, Jr. and Carolyn Bessette held their wedding reception. (The couple was married in the First African Baptist Church on the north end of the island.)

The trip to Cumberland Island takes about 6½ hours from Atlanta. Take I-75 to Macon, then I-16 east to Savannah. From Savannah take I-95 south approximately 90 miles to the St. Mary's exit.

The island is accessible only by ferry, and the number of visitors is limited to 300 per day. A visitor center and most of the historic sites are found at the southern end of the island, near the ferry dock. For reservations and fare information, call ☎ 912-882-4335.

THE GOLDEN ISLES
St. Simons, Jekyll, Sea Island and
Little St. Simons Island
Georgia Tourism Board
☎ 800-847-4842, www.georgia.org
800-933-COAST (2627)

St. Simons, Jekyll Island, Sea Island and Little St. Simons were first called "golden" by the Spanish.

Today, resorts and historic sites carry on the tradition. From Brunswick, 70 miles south of Savannah and 242 miles southeast of Atlanta, St. Simons and Jekyll are reached by causeways. Sea Island is bridged to St. Simons; and Little St. Simons, a private retreat, is reached only by boat.

All of the islands are great for walking along the beaches, wide expanses facing the Atlantic that transport you to another world. Spend hours shelling (whelks and conchs), and searching for sand dollars.

The islands are all quite different from one another, St. Simons the most touristy, Jekyll more of a quiet family-style retreat, and Little St. Simons for the upscale visitor. There are lots of amenities, such as good hotels, golf courses and a plethora of really good seafood restaurants.

From Atlanta, take I-75 south to Macon. Pick up I-16 east to Savannah and then I-95 south to the Brunswick exit, where you will get on 84 east to the Golden Isles.

West

BIRMINGHAM, ALABAMA

This Alabama city only 2½ hours from Atlanta (take I-20 west for 145 miles) has worked very hard to entice tourists in recent years by adding such attractions as **VisionLand**, a Six-Flags-style theme park, and the **McWane Center**, a science and technology museum. Other must-see sites include the **Birmingham Civil Rights Institute** and the **Birmingham Museum of Art**.

VisionLand Theme Park (☎ 205-481-4750) is near the town of Bessemer, Alabama, just outside of Bir-

Beyond Atlanta

mingham (continue on I-20 past Birmingham to reach Bessemer). Admission is $22 for adults and $18 for children and seniors; the park is open weekends only between April 10-May 31, and daily from 10 am-10 pm between May 31-August 21.

The McWane Center is housed in a renovated department store in Birmingham, at 200 19th Street North (☎ 205-714-8300). The center is open Mondays-Saturdays, 10 am-5 pm, and Sundays, noon-5 pm; admission is $7 for adults, $6 for seniors and youths under 13, $5 for children under five, and free for children under three.

The Birmingham Civil Rights Institute (☎ 205-328-9696) is at 520 16th Street North, in the Civil Rights District. Admission to the Institute is $5 for adults, $2 for seniors, and $1 for college students. Hours are Tuesdays-Saturdays, 10 am-5 pm, and Sundays, 1-5 pm. Nearby are the 16th Street Baptist Church, Kelly Ingram Park, and the Alabama Jazz Hall of Fame.

For more information about attractions, contact the Birmingham Convention & Visitors Bureau at ☎ 800-962-6453, or www.birminghamal.org.

US SPACE & ROCKET CENTER
One Tranquility Base
Huntsville, AL 35807
☎ 256-837-3400 or 800-637-7223 (for reservations); www.ussrc.com

Home to the US Space Camp, US Space Academy, Aviation Challenge and the NASA Visitor Center, this is an interactive, first-class day of fun. Displays from the US Space program, space travel simulators and an IMAX theater are just a few of the highlights.

Huntsville is in northern Alabama, about 3½ hours from Atlanta. Take I-20 west to Highway 431 north into Huntsville.

Northwest

ETOWAH INDIAN MOUNDS
813 Indian Mounds Road
Cartersville, GA
Admission: $3 for adults, $2 for ages six-18, under six free
Hours: Tuesdays-Saturdays, 9:00 am-5:30 pm; Sundays, 2:00-5:30 pm
☎ 770-387-3747

Home to a flourishing Etowah Indian community from AD 1000 to 1500, these ceremonial mounds were used as burial places, priests platforms and temples. The largest of the three grassy mounds stands 63 feet tall. This is a registered State Historic Site.

Cartersville is about 45 miles northwest of Atlanta. take I-75 north; turn left on Highway 20 and left again on Highway 61, and follow the signs from there.

Atlanta A-Z

Airport Information & Transportation

Hartsfield Atlanta Int'l Airport . . . . . ☎ 404-530-6830

Atlanta Airport Shuttle . . . . ☎ 404-766-5312

Atlanta Hotels Connection . . . . ☎ 404-312-2479

Daytime Transportation . . . . ☎ 404-399-6069

MARTA . . . . ☎ 404-848-4711

Amtrak . . . . ☎ 404-881-3062 or 800-872-7245

Babysitting

Ask your hotel concierge to recommend a service.

Banks/ATMs

Plentiful locations all around the town. Be careful in the evening as most are not enclosed and offer little protection. Service charges for using an ATM in Atlanta are normally $1.50 per transaction.

First Union . . . . ☎ 800-275-3862, ext 3

Southtrust . . . . ☎ 770-951-4000

Suntrust . . . . ☎ 404-230-5555

Wachovia . . . . ☎ 404-332-5000

Bus Service

MARTA . . . . ☎ 404-848-4711

MARTA Handicapped Services ..... ☎ 404-848-5389

Greyhound .... ☎ 404-584-1731 or 800-231-2222

Dentists

The **Georgia Dental Association of Atlanta** (☎ 404-636-7553), open weekdays from 8:30-5, can refer you to a dentist close to your hotel, or to one who can best accommodate your needs.

Doctors

The **Medical Association of Atlanta** (☎ 404-881-1714) offers a referral service for various specialties.

Emergencies

Emergencies (police, fire or ambulance) .... ☎ 911

Ambulance .... ☎ 404-521-4141 or 521-3661

City of Atlanta Fire Dept............. ☎ 404-659-2121

City of Atlanta Police .... ☎ 404-658-6600

Hospitals

Piedmont Hospital
1968 Peachtree Street .... ☎ 404- 350-2222

Georgia Baptist Medical Center
303 Parkway...................... ☎ 404-265-4000

Grady Memorial Hospital
80 Butler Street .... ☎ 404-616-4307

Crawford Long Hospital
550 Peachtree Street................. ☎ 404-686-4411

Newspapers

The *Atlanta Constitution* and the *Atlanta Journal* (both owned by the same company) publish daily; ☎ 404-526-5151.

Pharmacies

CVS Drugs offers 24-hour service at some locations; ☎ 404-881-0329.

Pharmacies at **Kroger Grocers** are open 9 am-9 pm; ☎ 404-237-8022.

Rental Car Agencies

National Car Rental Agencies

Alamo	☎ 800-327-9633
Avis	☎ 800-331-1212
Budget	☎ 800-527-0700
Dollar	☎ 800-800-4000
Hertz	☎ 800-654-3131
National	☎ 800-227-7368
Payless	☎ 800-729-3577
Thrifty	☎ 800-367-2277
Value	☎ 800-468-2583

Local Car Rental Agencies

Atlanta Rent-A-Car	☎ 770-448-6066
Rent-A-Wreck	☎ 404-363-8720

Atlanta A-Z

Taxi Service

Buckhead Safety Cab. . . . . ☎ 404-233-1152

Checker Cab . . . . ☎ 404-351-1111

Executive Limousine . . . . ☎ 404-223-2000

Southern Taxi & Limo . . . . ☎ 404-633-0030

Telephone Service

In Atlanta you must dial the area code even if you are calling a number within the same area code. Currently, pay telephones cost 35¢ per call. Be sure to have exact change as the telephones cannot make change.

Transit Authorities

Cobb Community Transit . . . . ☎ 770-427-4444

MARTA Bus & Rail System . . . . ☎ 404-848-4711

MARTA Handicapped Services . . . . . ☎ 404-848-5389

Web Sites

Alpharetta Conv & Vis Bur . . www.alpharettacvb.com

Atlanta Ballet . . . . www.atlantaballet.com

Atlanta Braves . . . . www.AtlantaBraves.com

Atlanta Conv & Vis Bur . . . . www.atlanta.com

Atlanta Festivals . . . . www.atlantafestivals.com

Atlanta Falcons. . . . . www.AtlantaFalcons.com

Atlanta Hawks . . . . www.nba.com/hawks

Atlanta Thrashers . . . . www.atlantathrashers.com

Atlanta Symphony . . . . www.atlantasymphony.org

Callanwolde Fine Arts Center. . www.callanwolde.org

Callaway Gardens . . . . www.callawaygardens.org

Civil War Museum . . . . . www.kennesawmountain.org

Cobb County CVB . . . . www.cobbcvb.com

Dahlonega Chbr. of Commerce. . . www.dahlonega.org

DeKalb County CVB . . . . www.atlantasdekalb.org

Dogwood Festival . . . . www.dogwood.org

Douglasville CVB . . . . www.douglasvillecvb.org

Gwinnett County CVB . . . . www.gcvb.org

High Museum of Art . . . . www.high.org

Margaret Mitchell House . . . . www.GWTW.org

Music Midtown Festival. . . . www.musicmidtown.com

Shakespeare Festival. . . . . . . www.gashakespeare.org

Stone Mountain Park . . www.stonemountainpark.com

Index